ABANDONED

VOLUME 3

Coco Key Waterpark - Rockford, IL

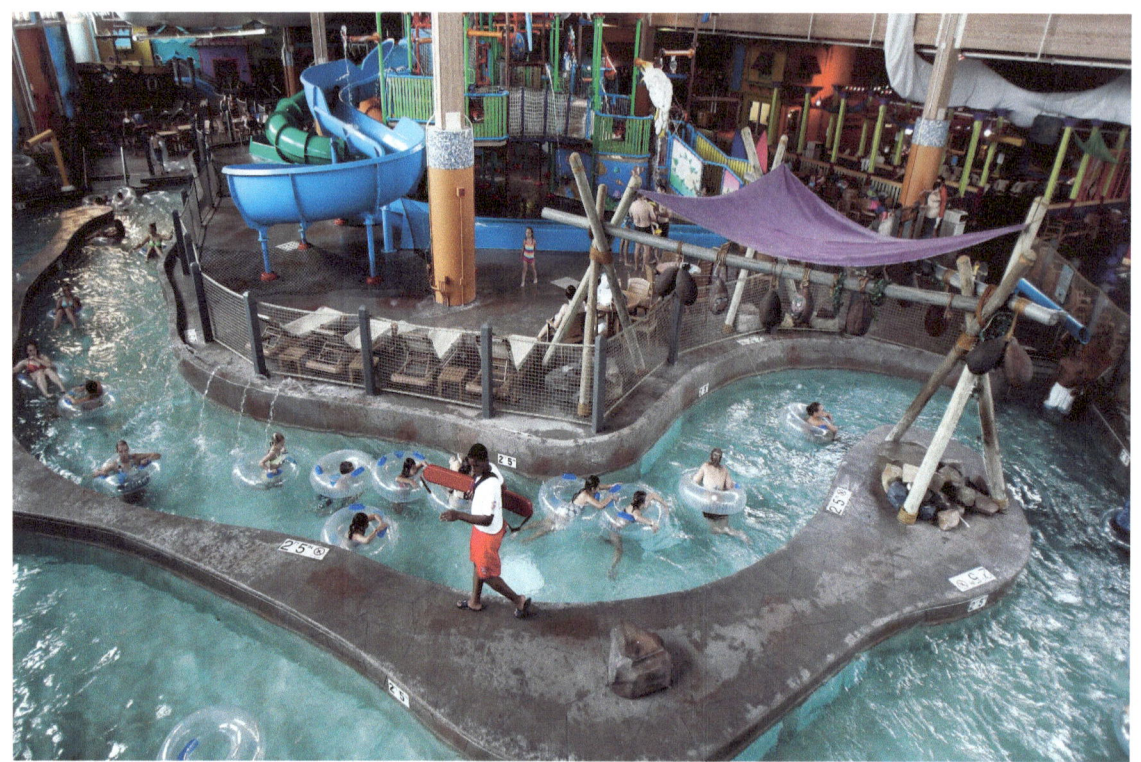

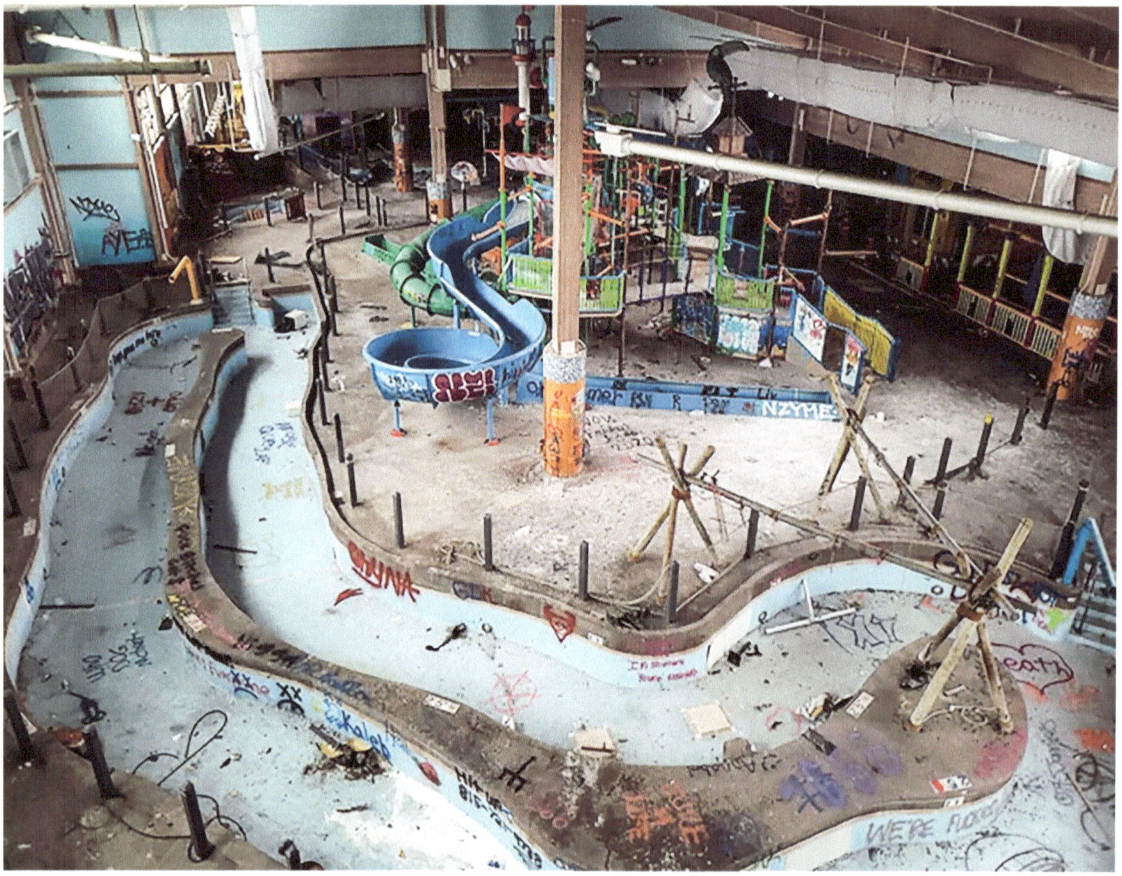

Bushkill Resort Theater - Poconos, NY

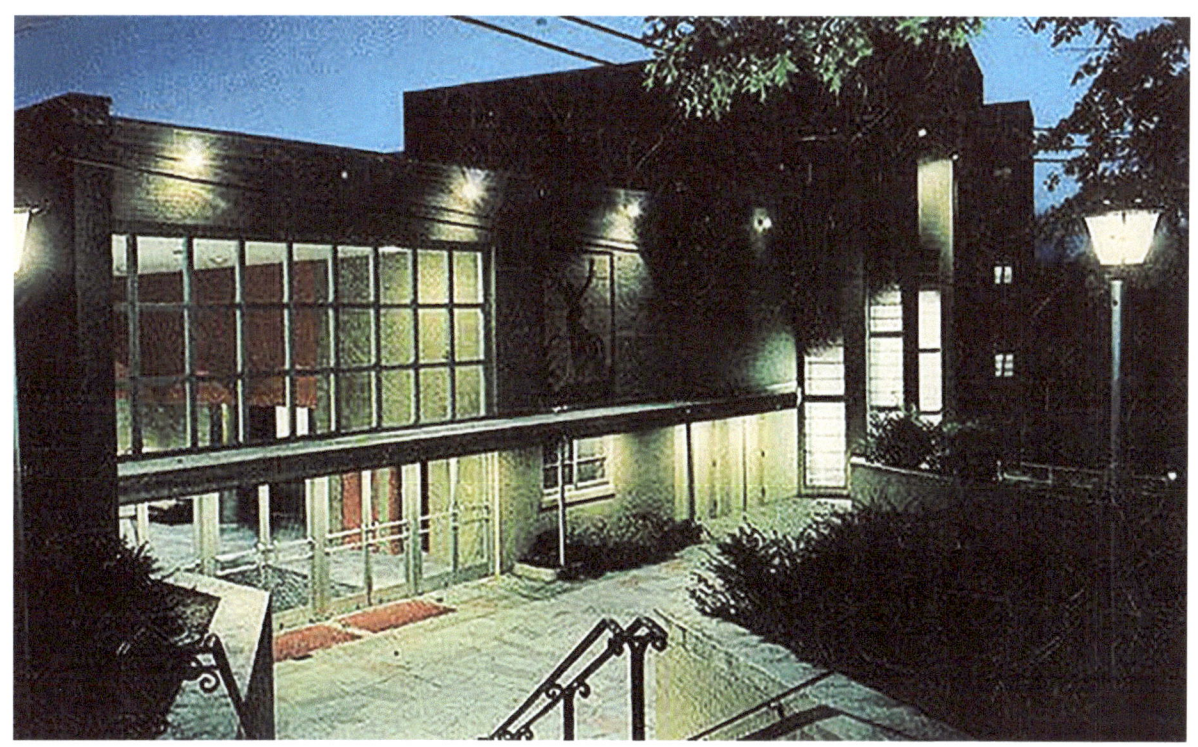

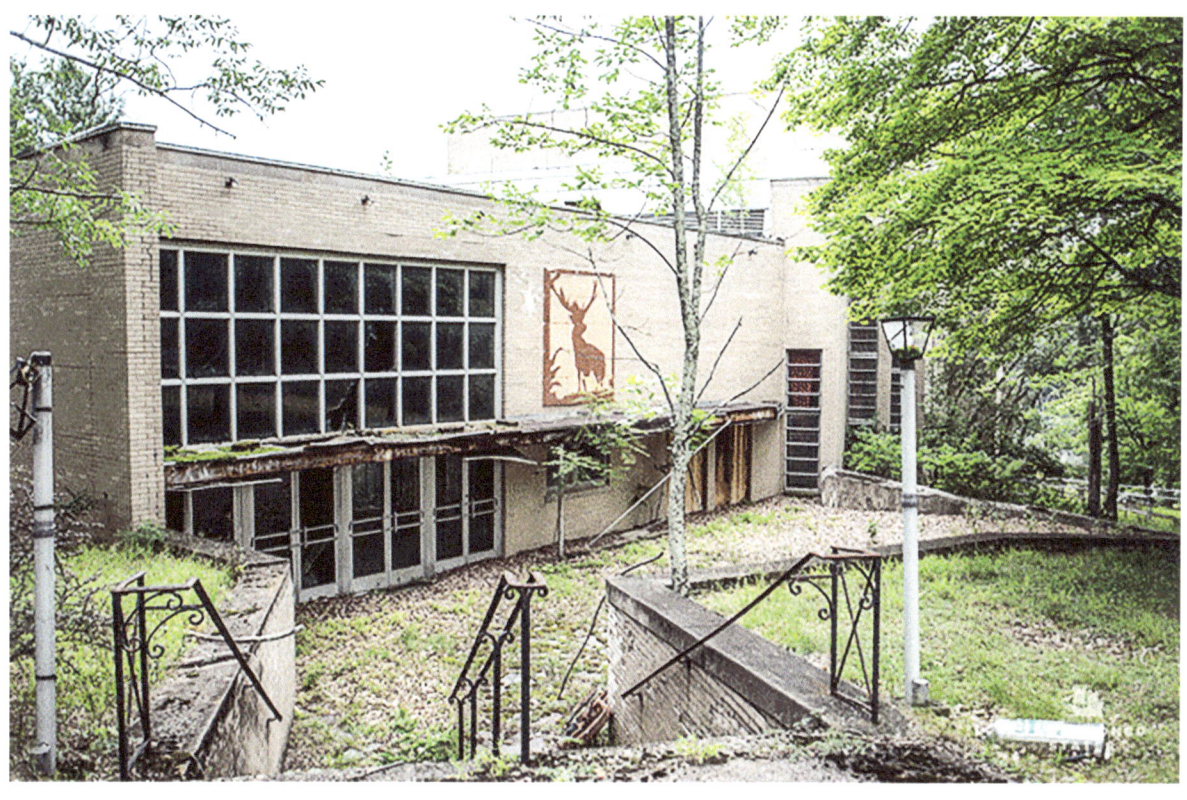

Capricorn International Resort
- Queensland, Australia

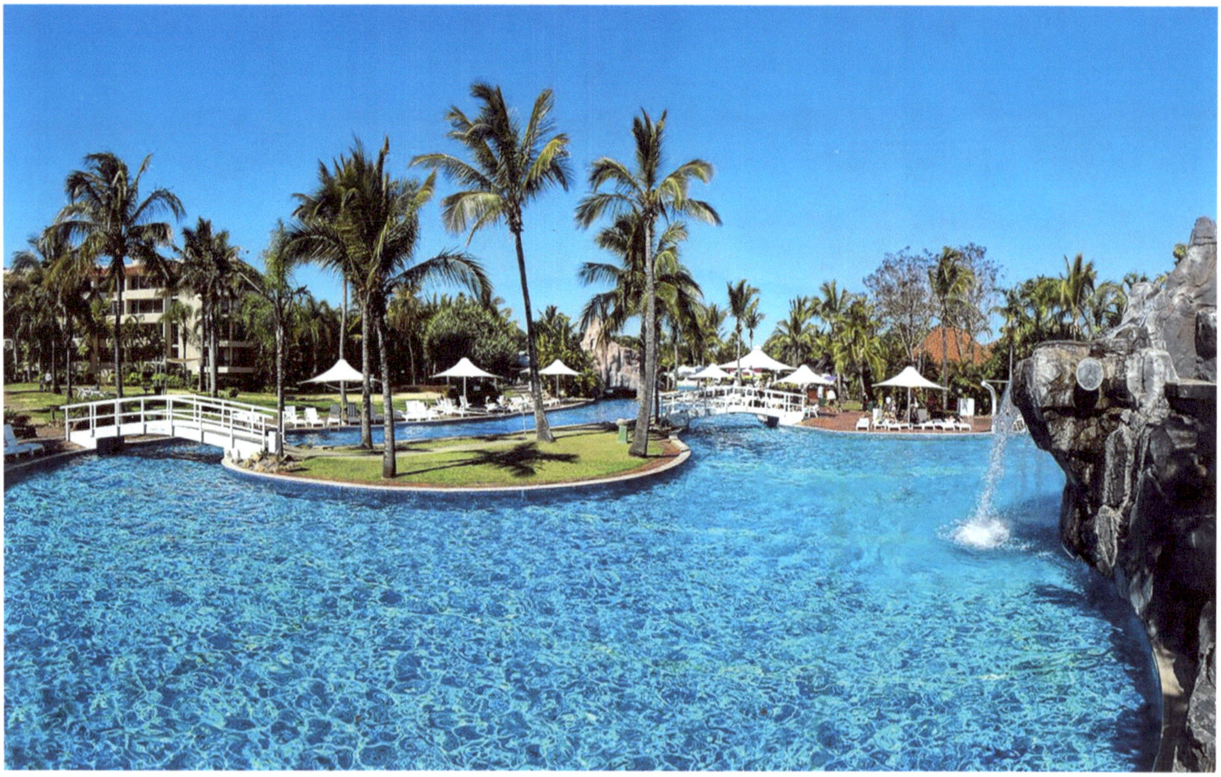

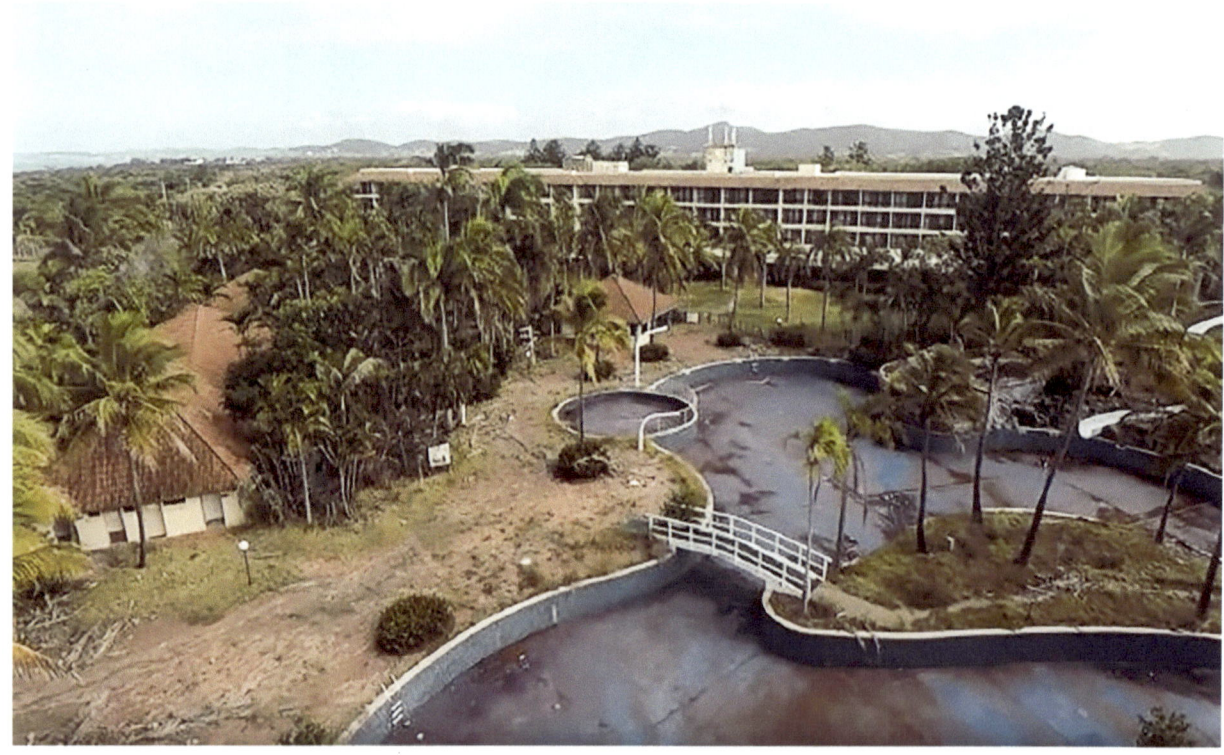

Château Marteau Longe - Belgium

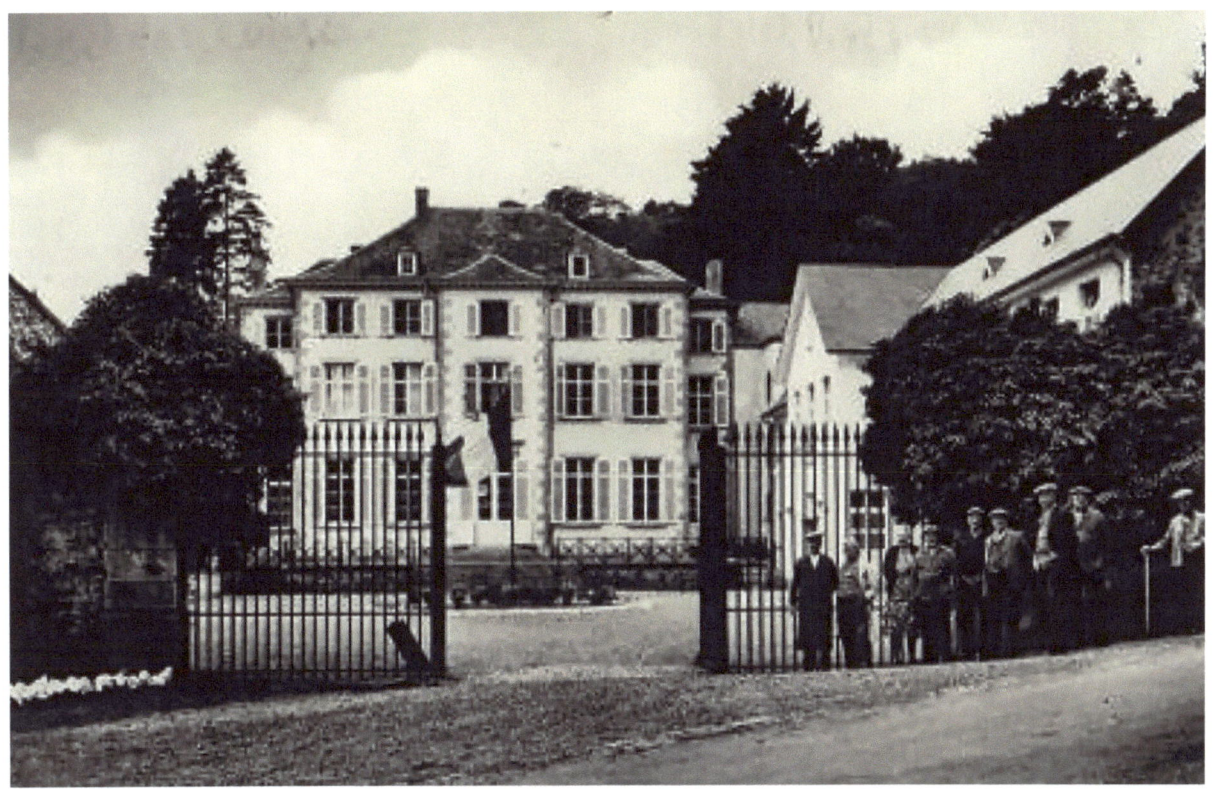

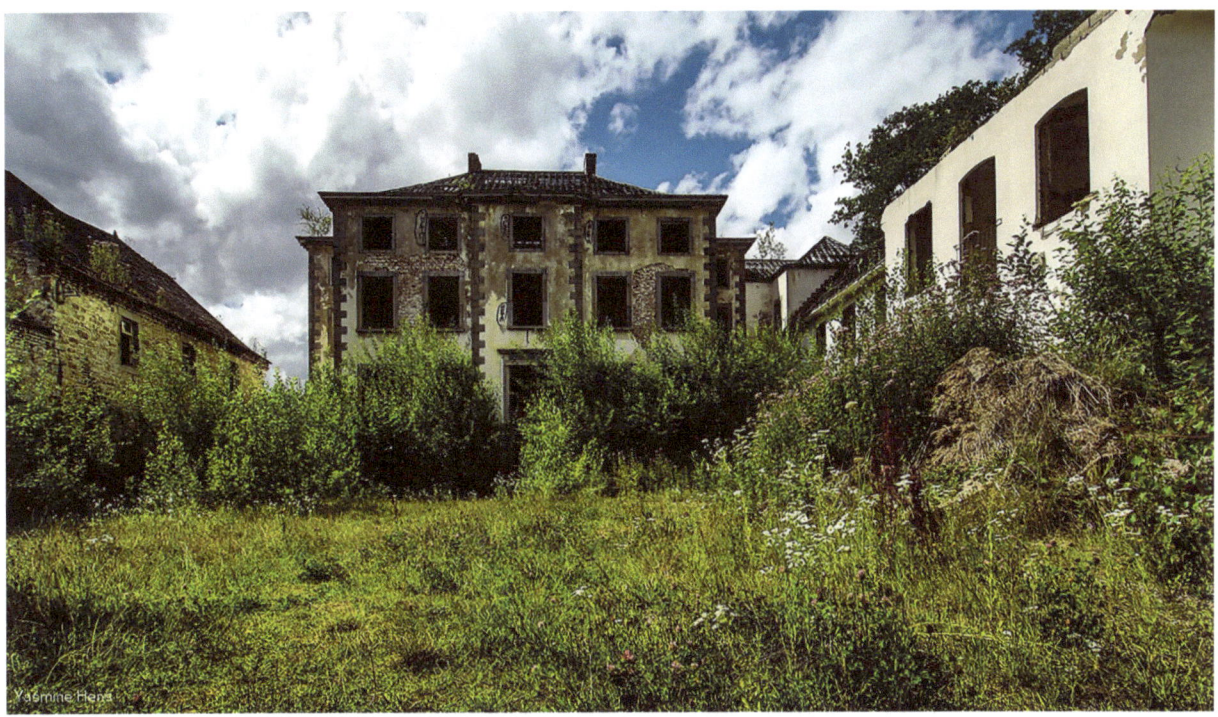

Chateau Nottebohm - Belgium

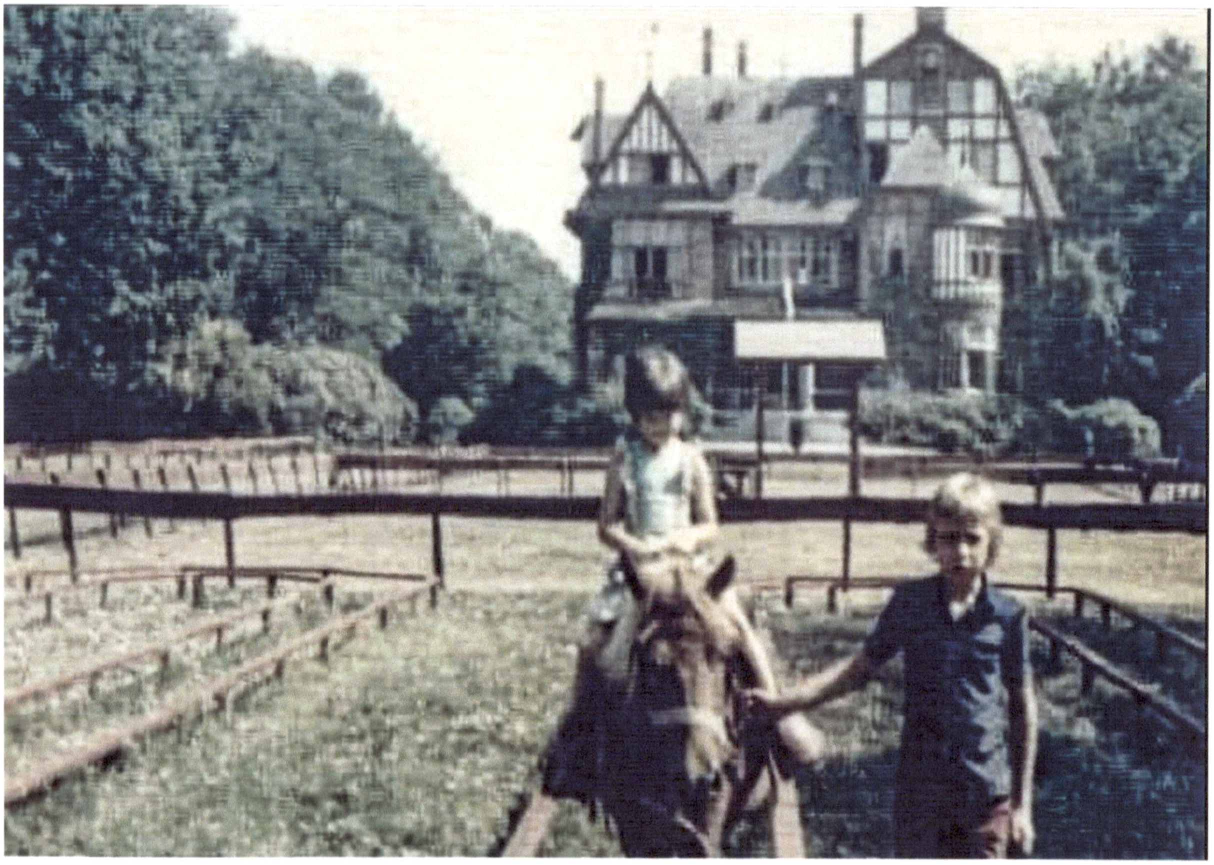

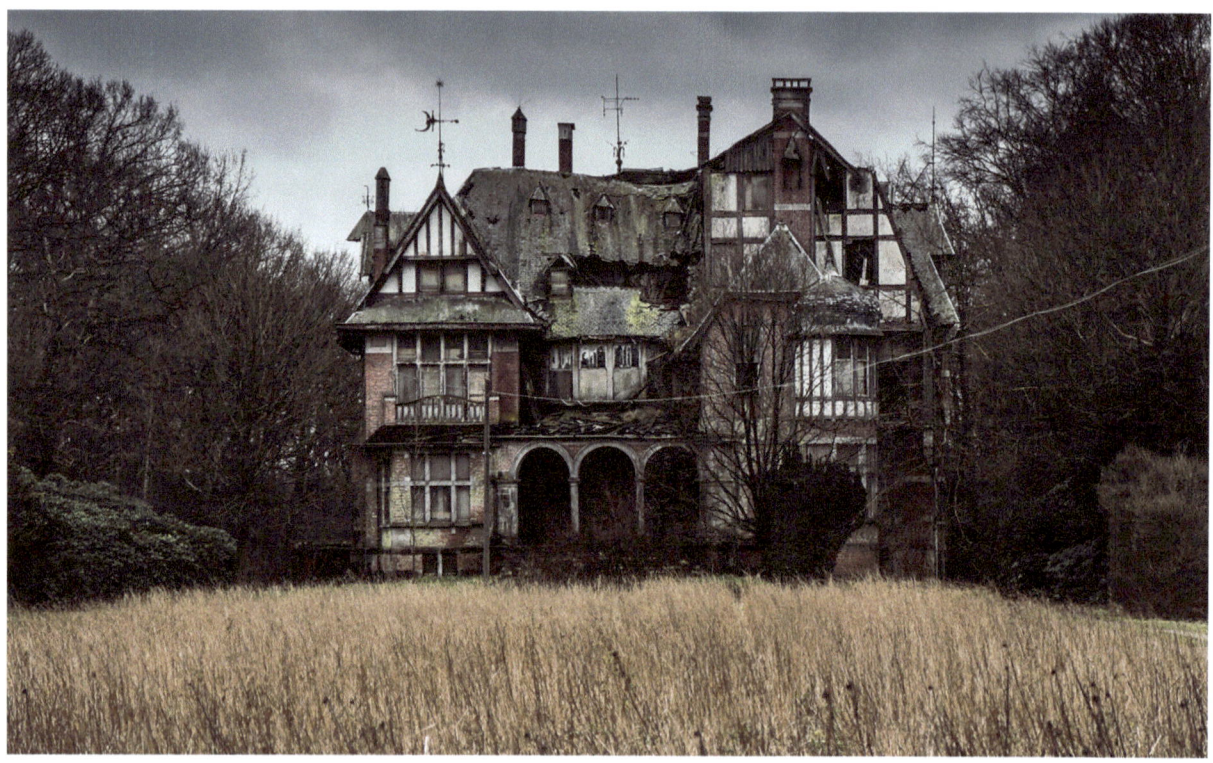

Chateau Nottebohm II - Belgium

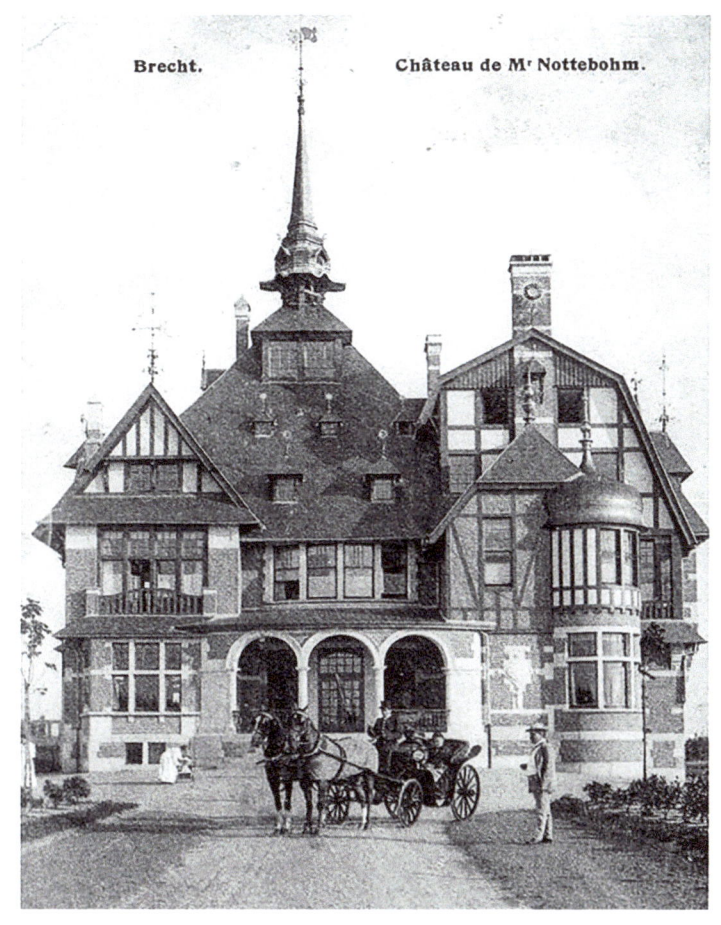

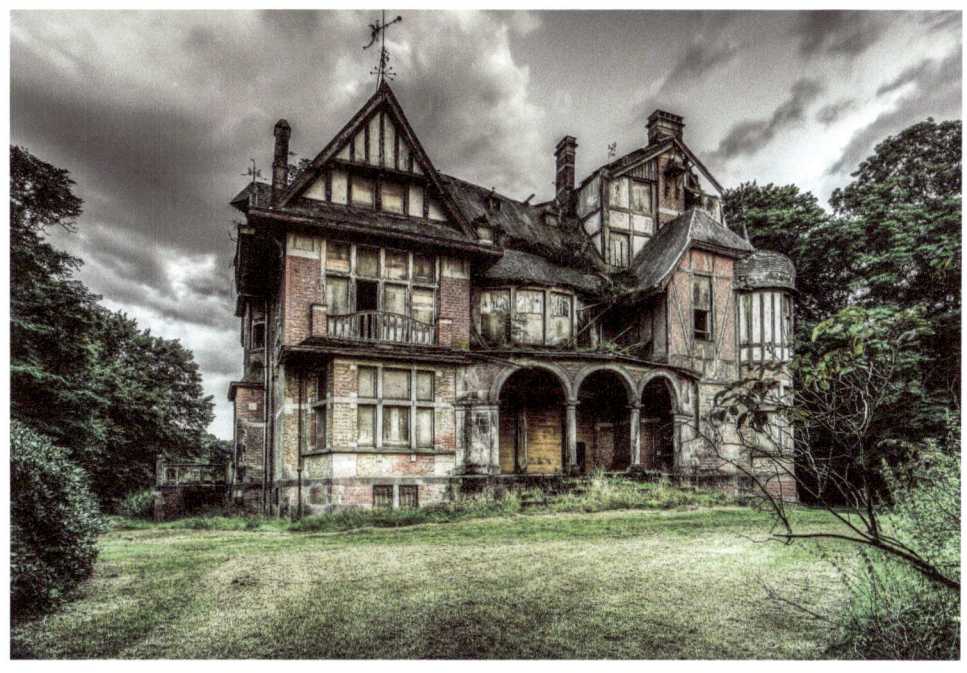

Chippewa Lake Amusement Park - OH

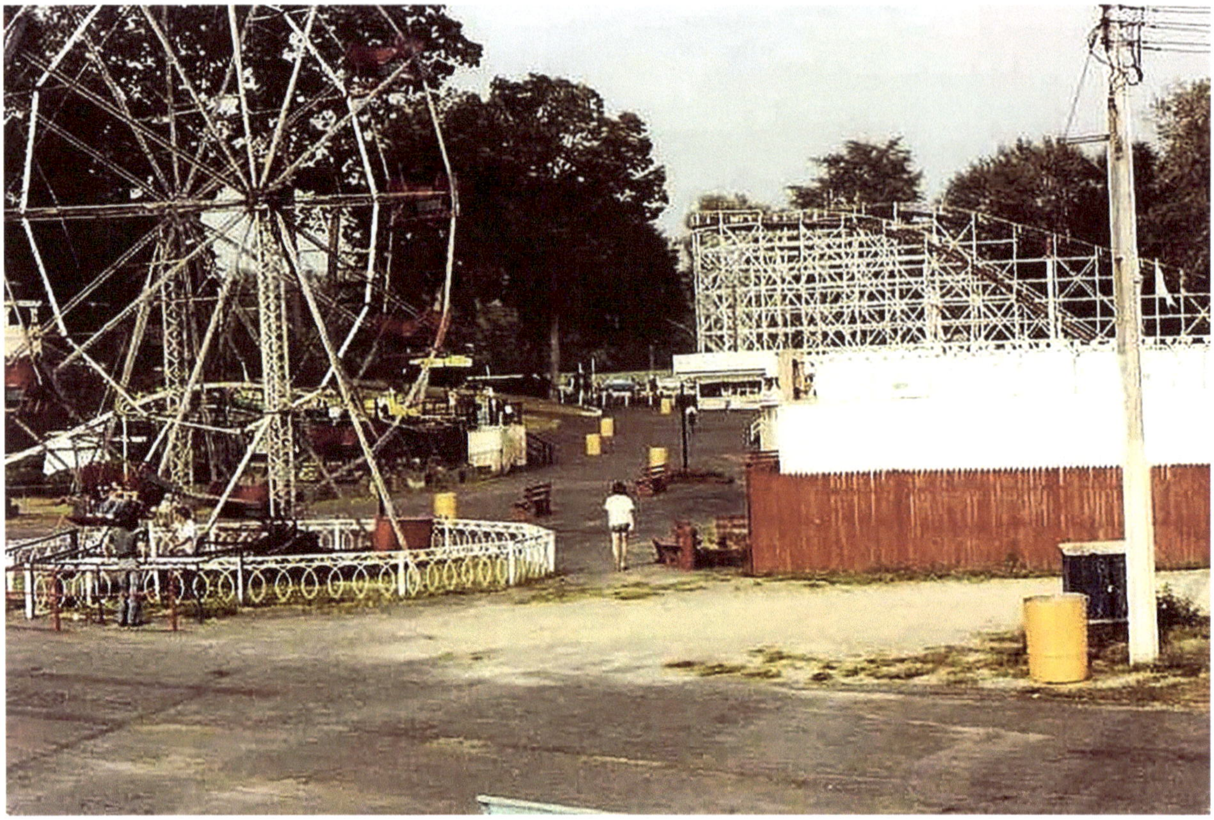

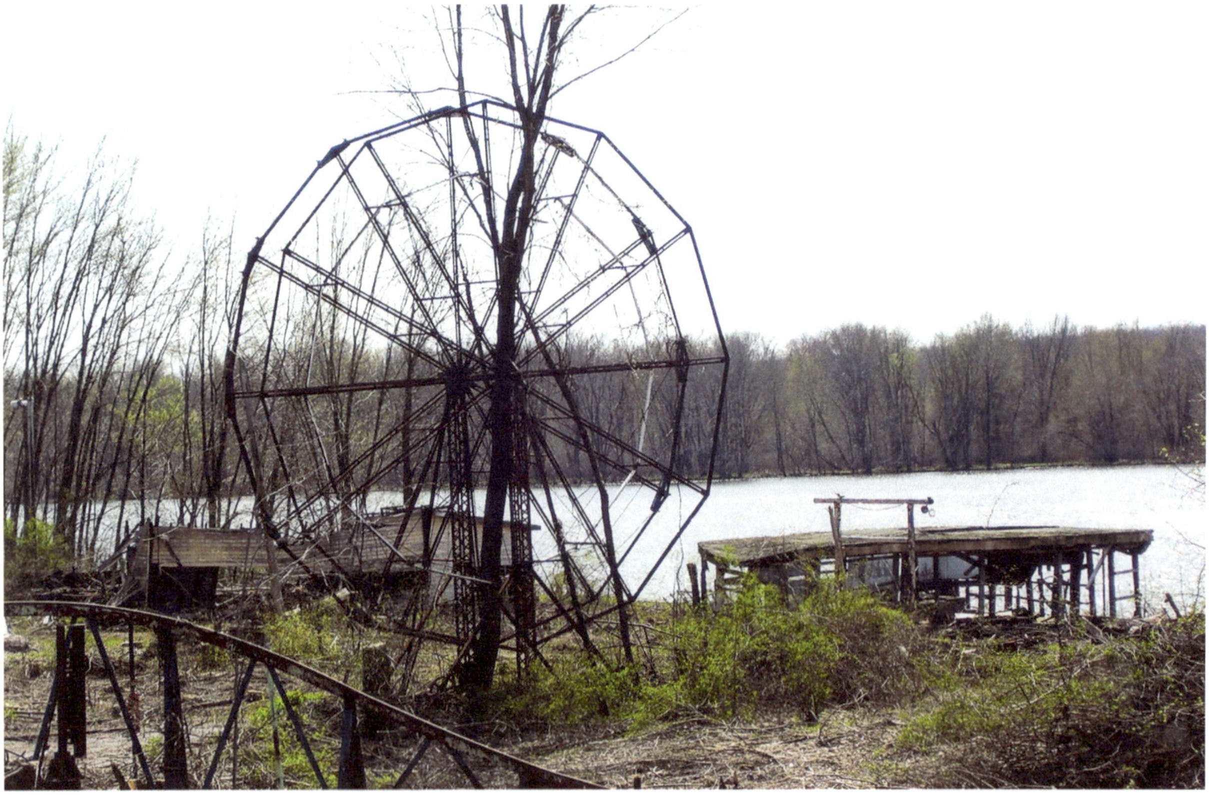

Clifton Rocks Railway - Bristol, England

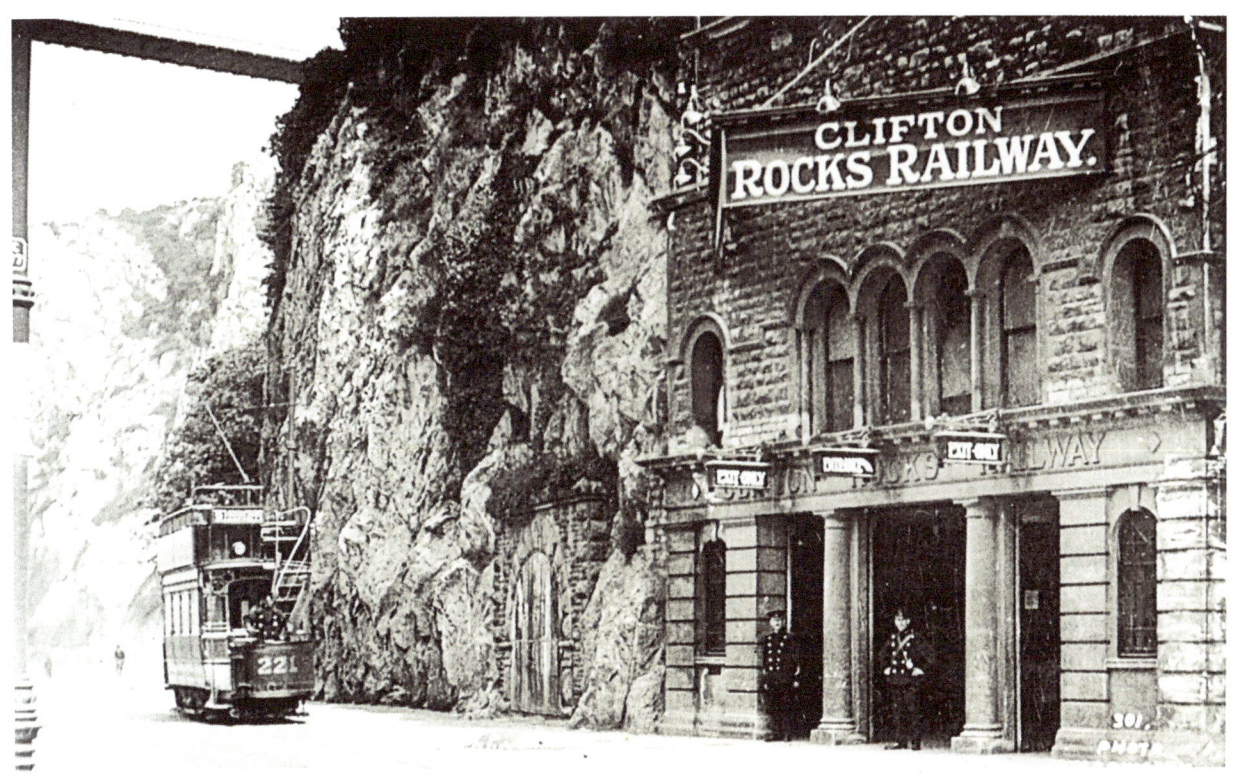

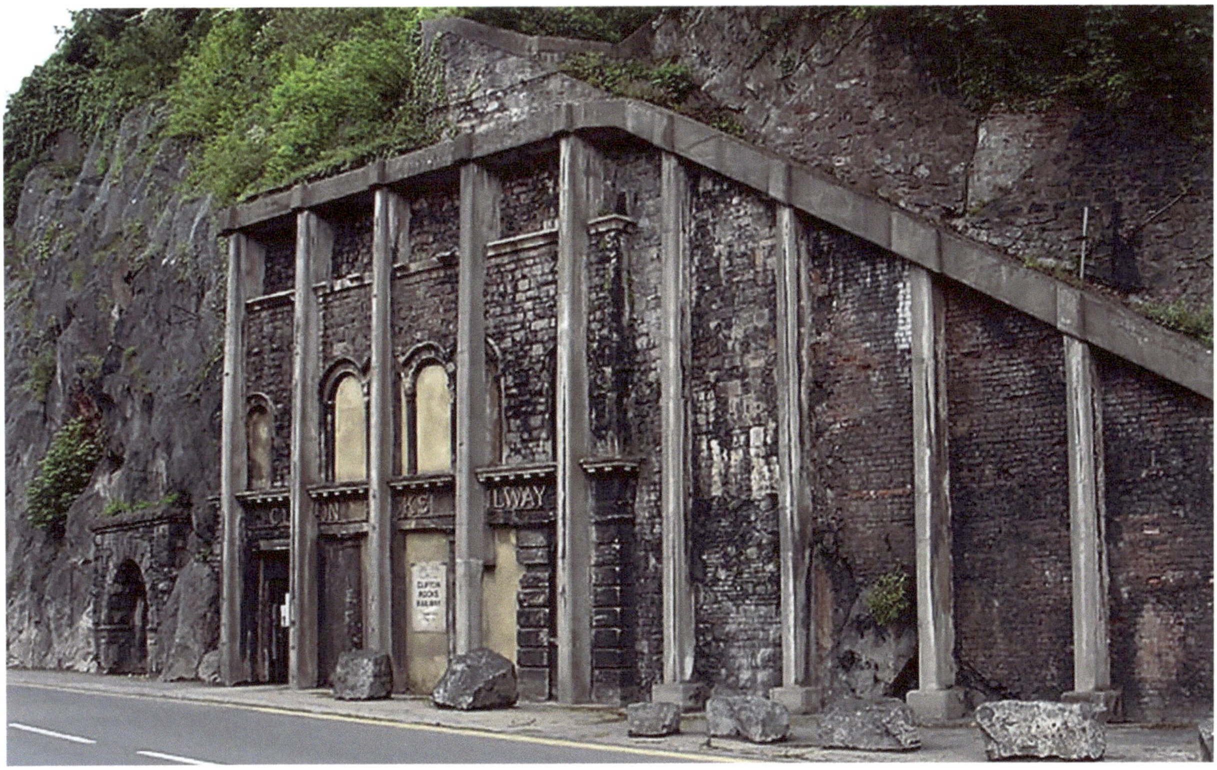

Amboy Cinemas - Sayreville, NJ

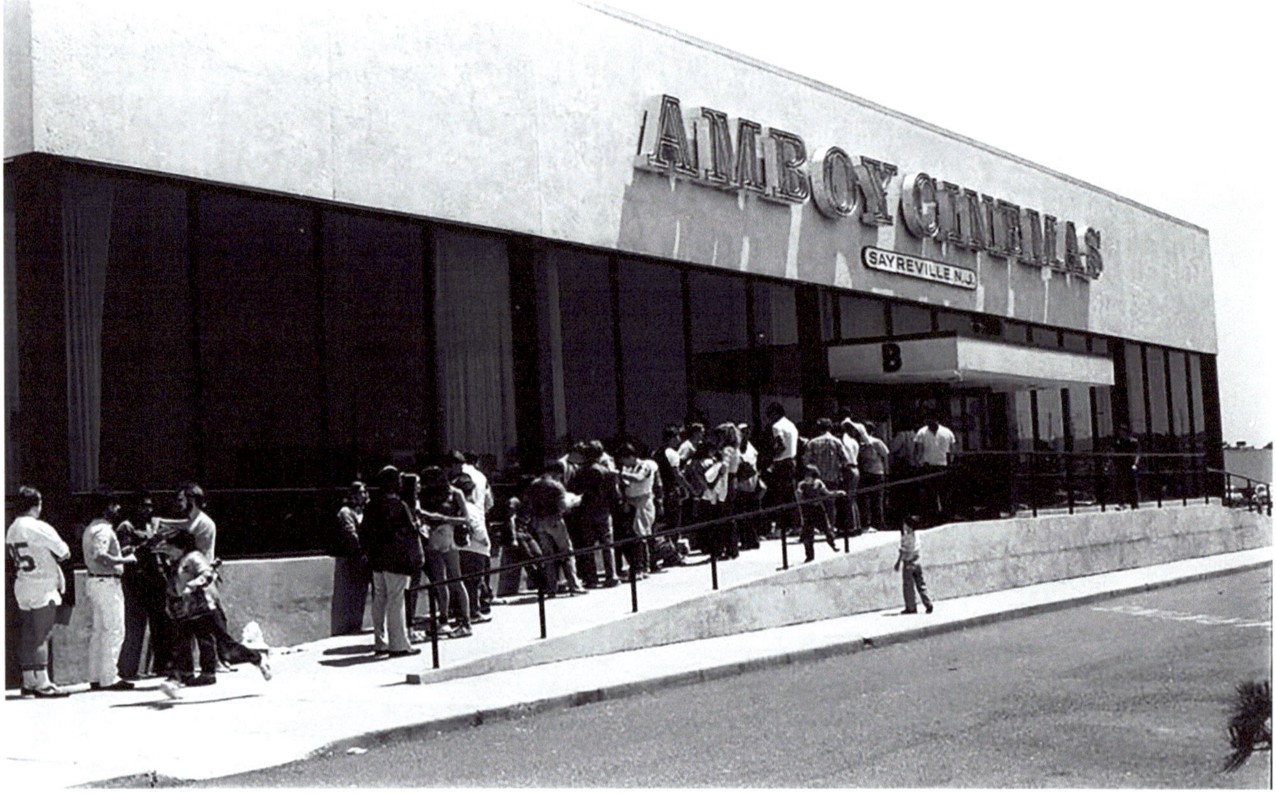

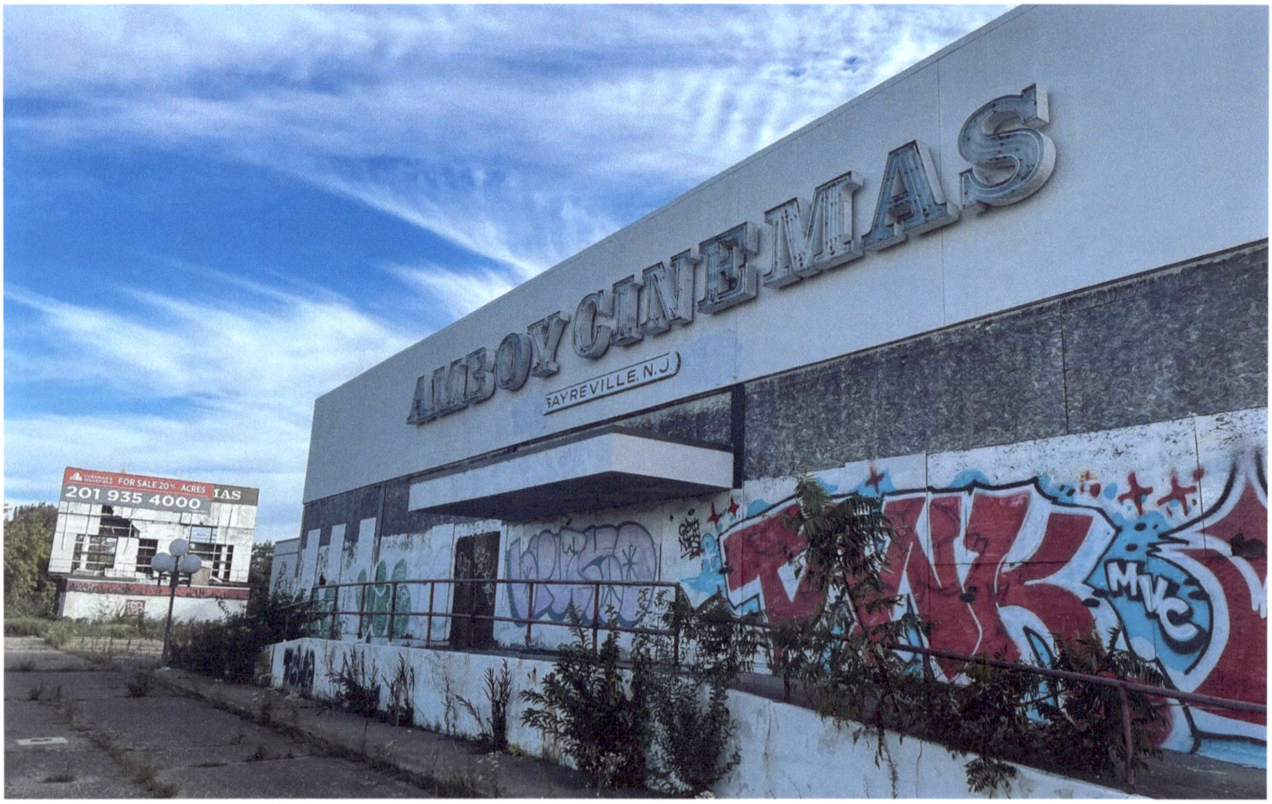

Club Maeva Tulum Resort - Mexico

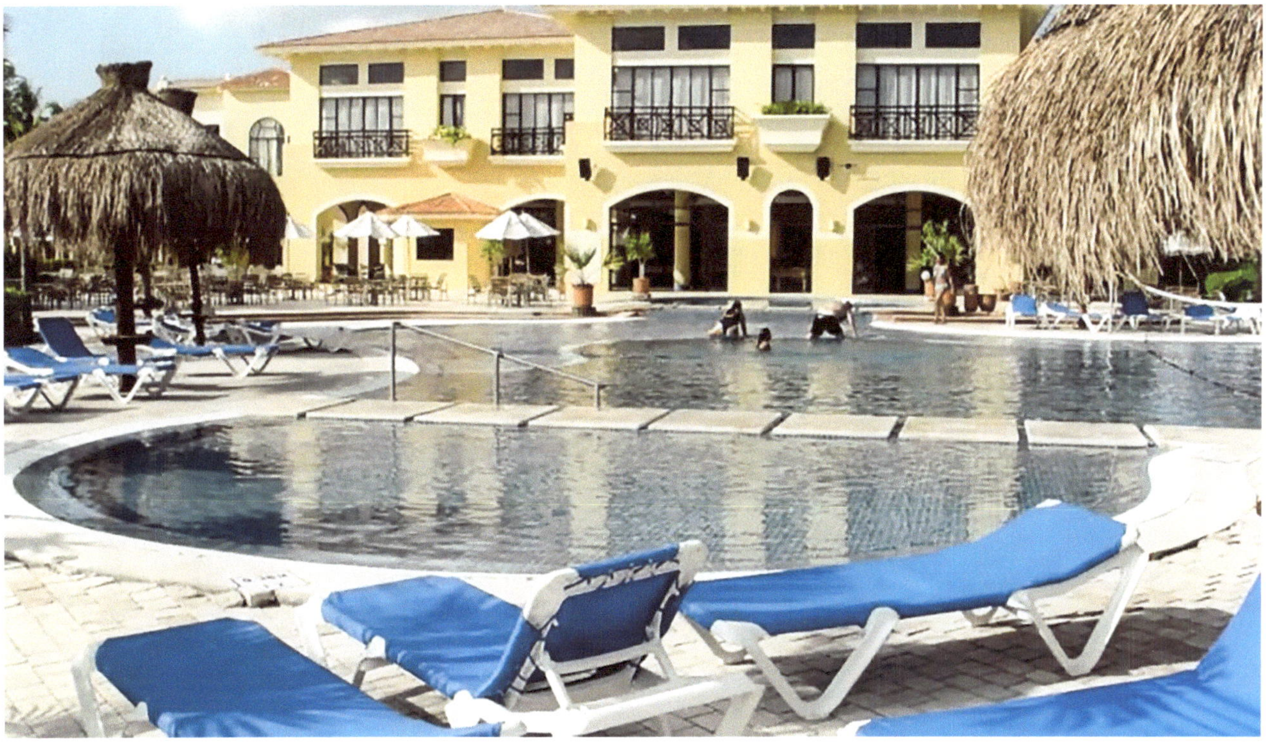

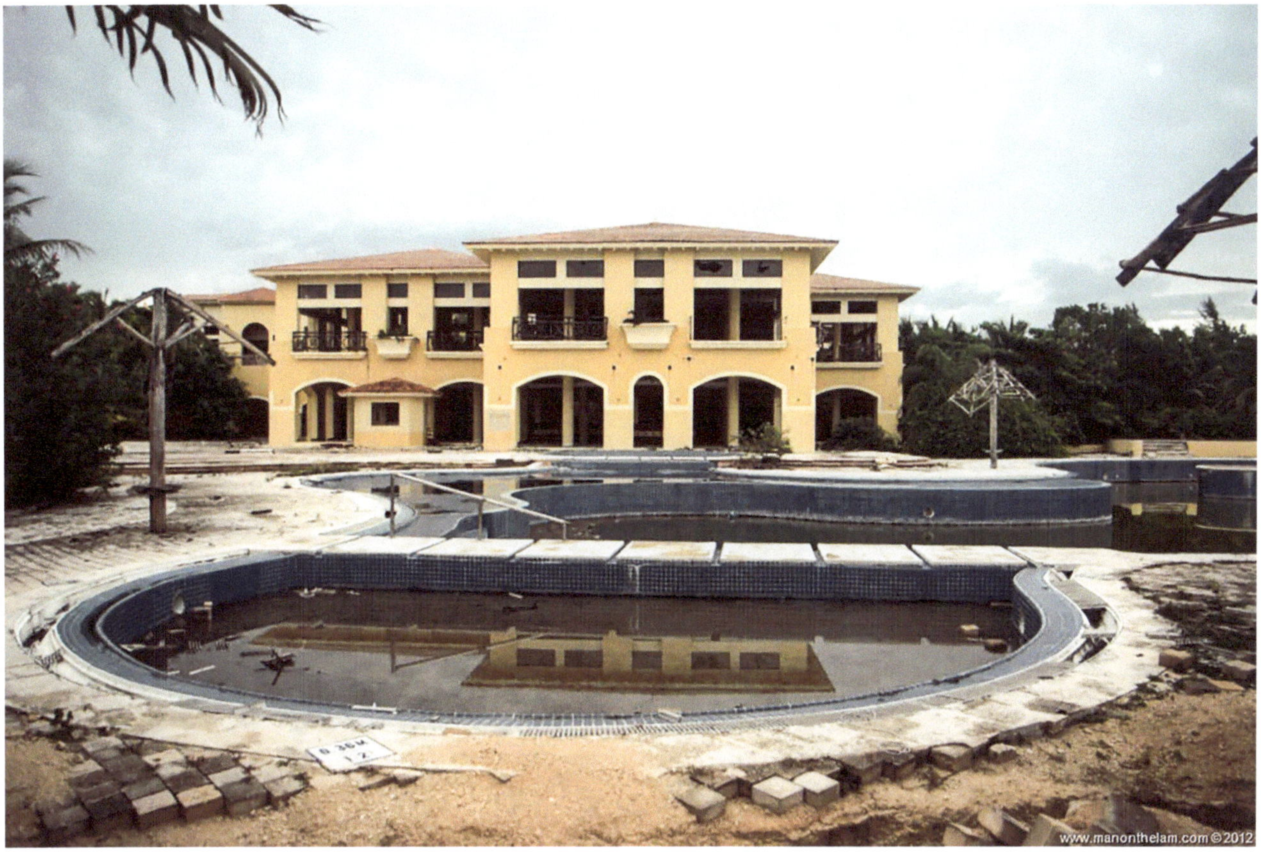

Collin Creek Mall - Plano, TX

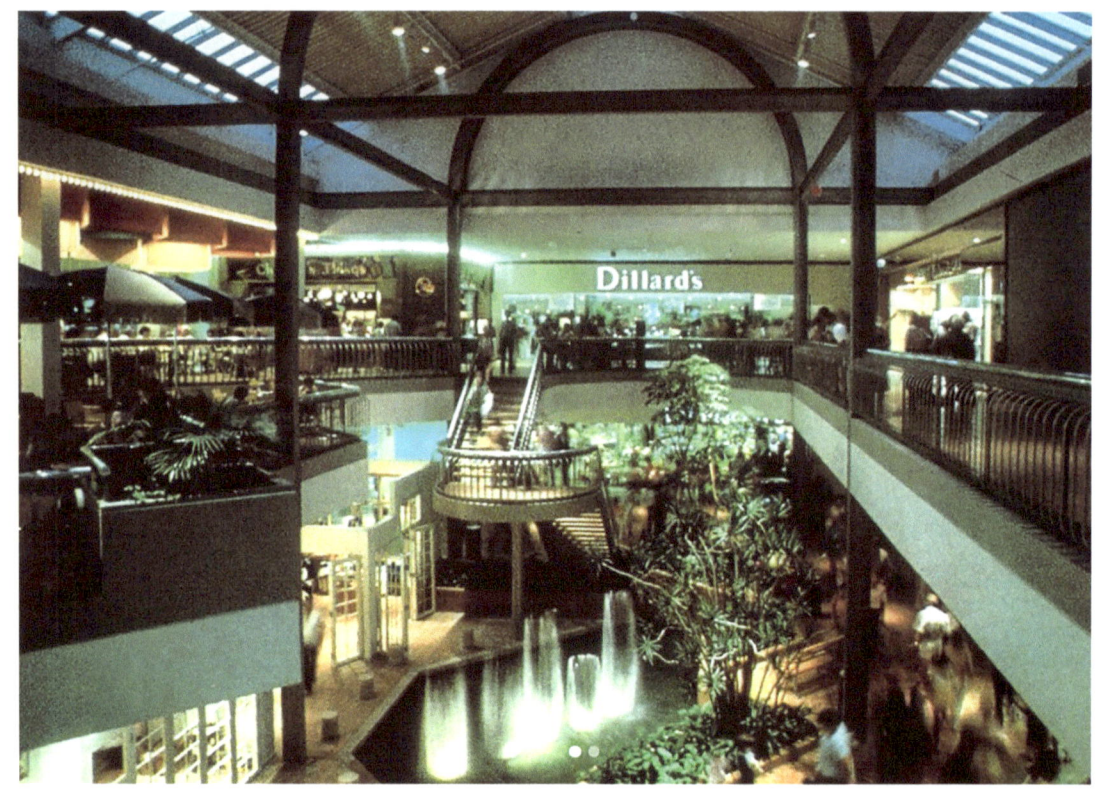

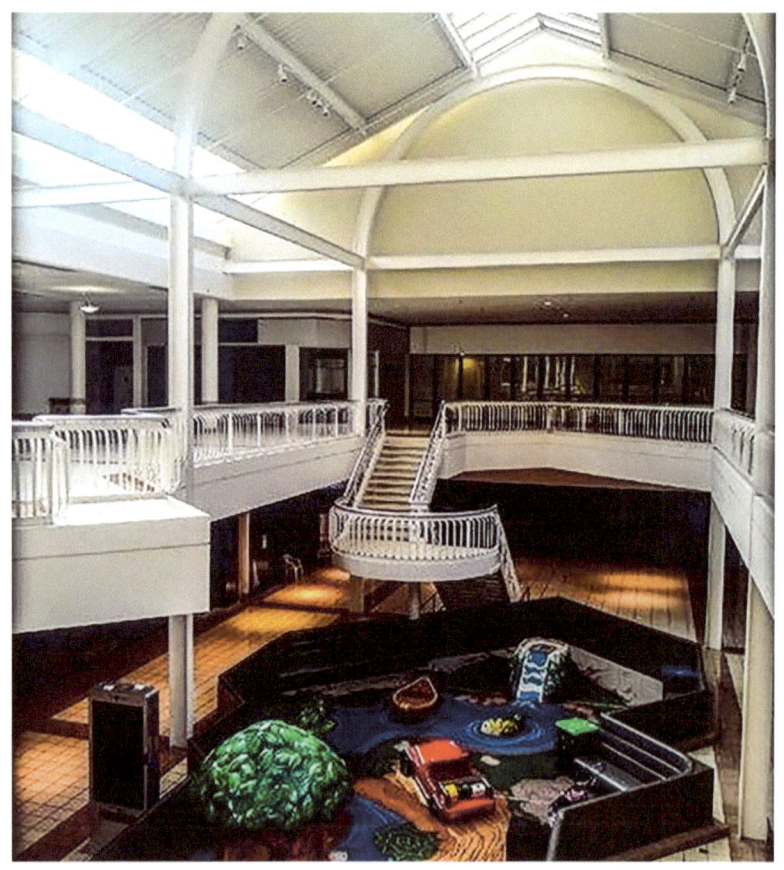

Apple Ridge Country Club - Mahwah, New Jersey

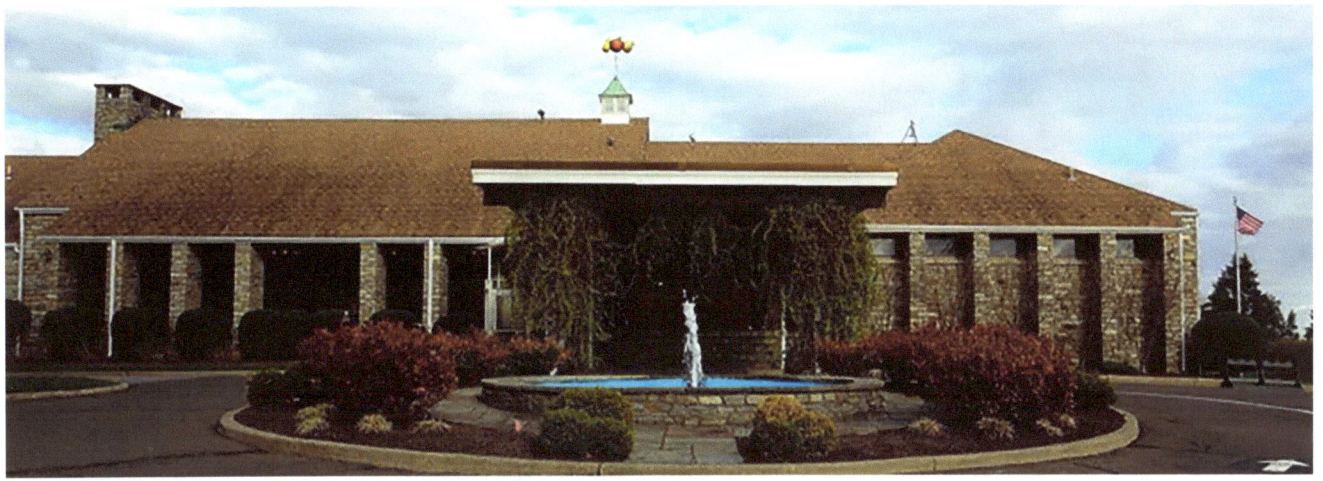

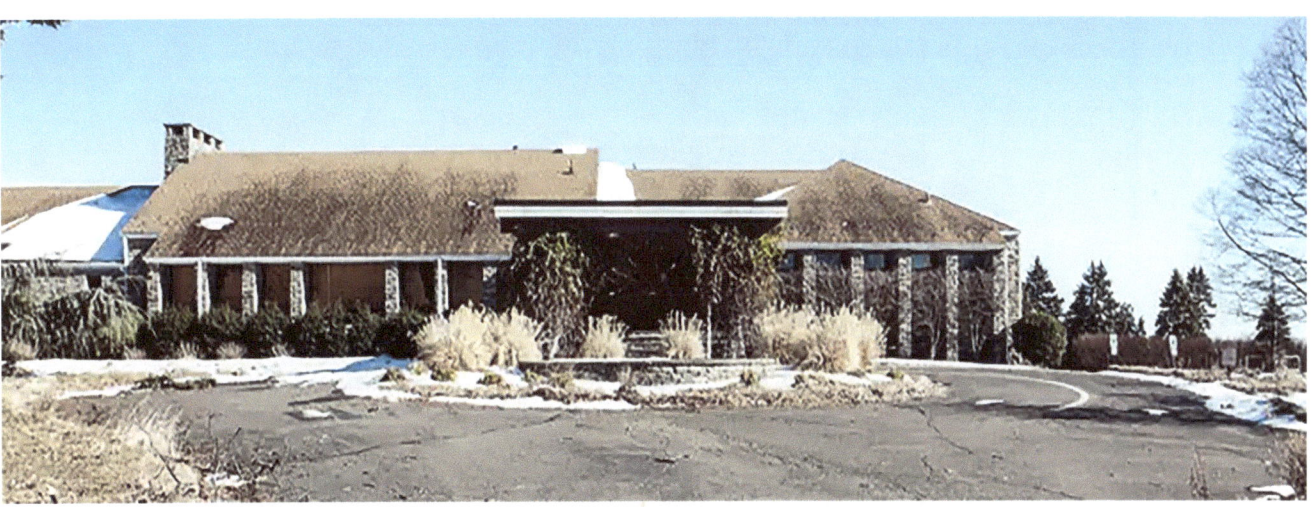

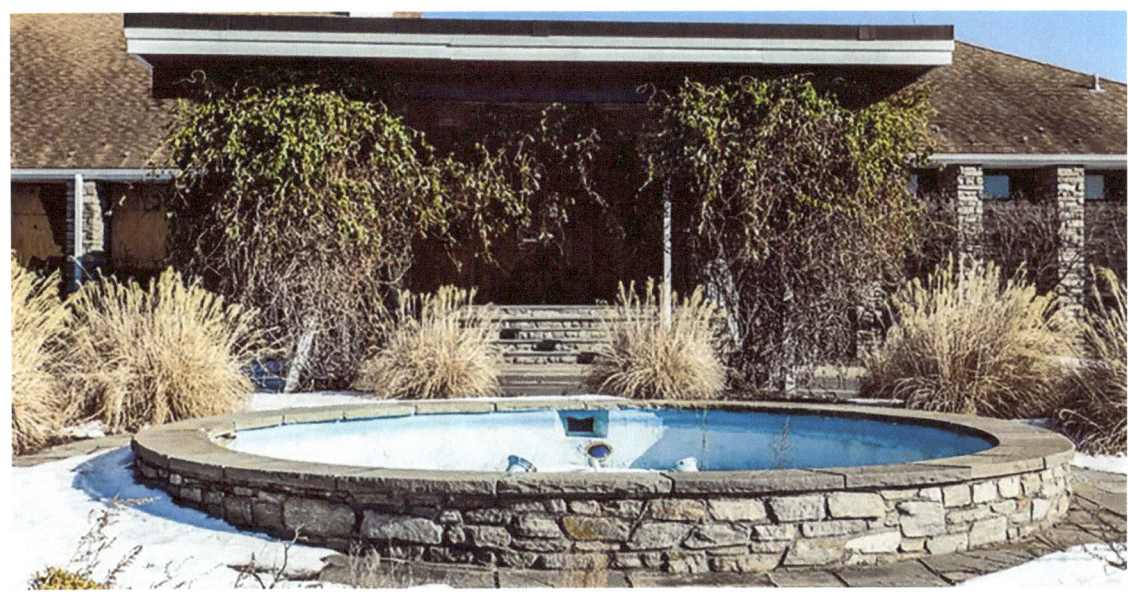

Detroit, Michigan - Dilapidated Neighborhood

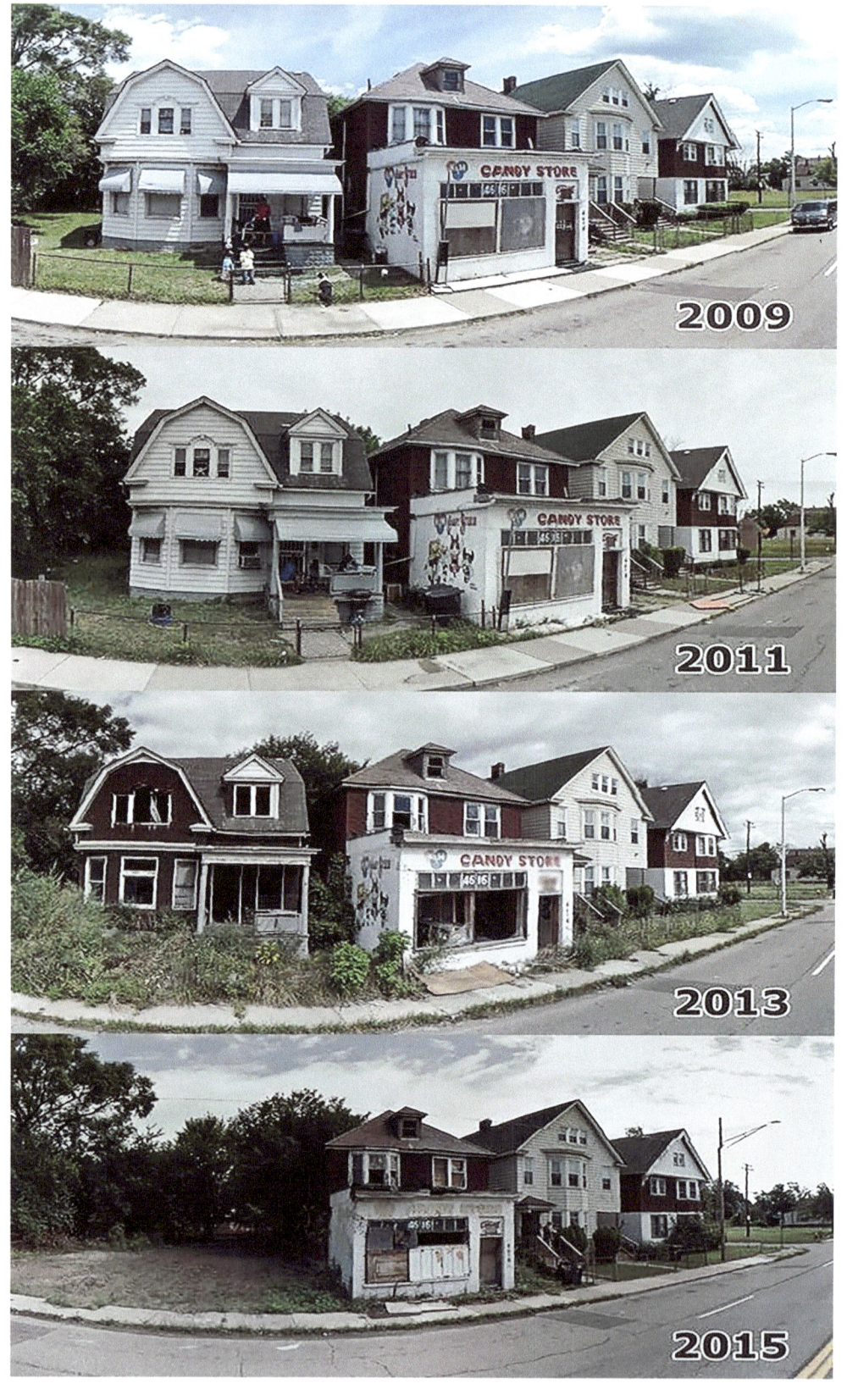

Eastown Theatre - Detroit, MI

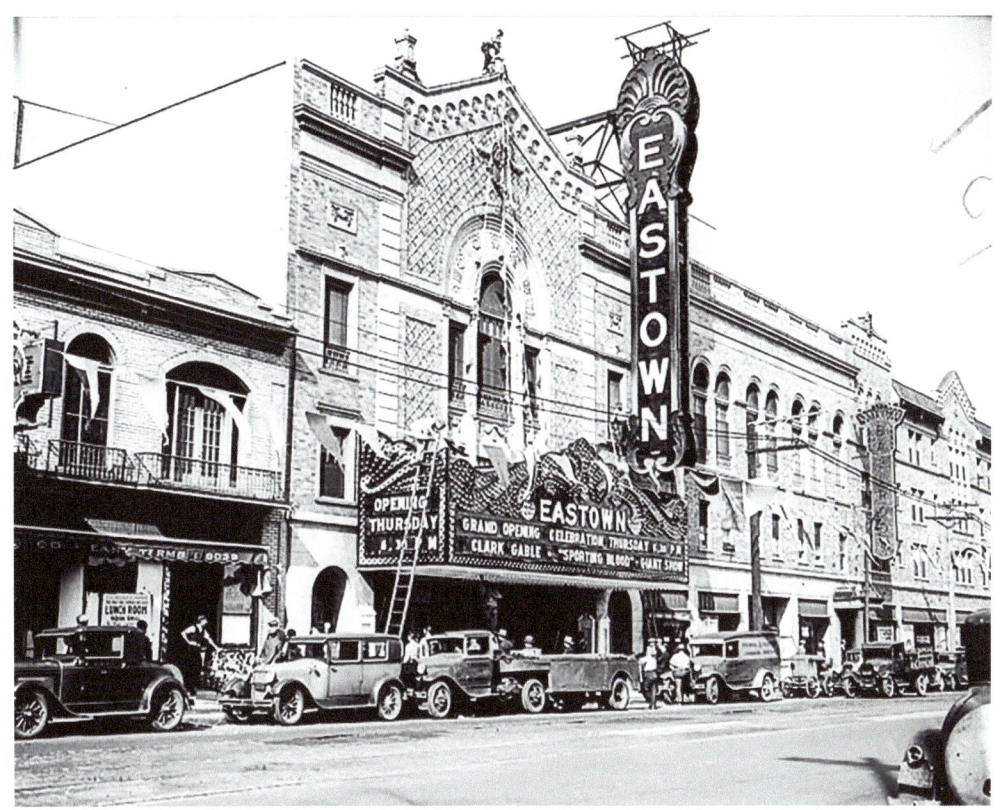

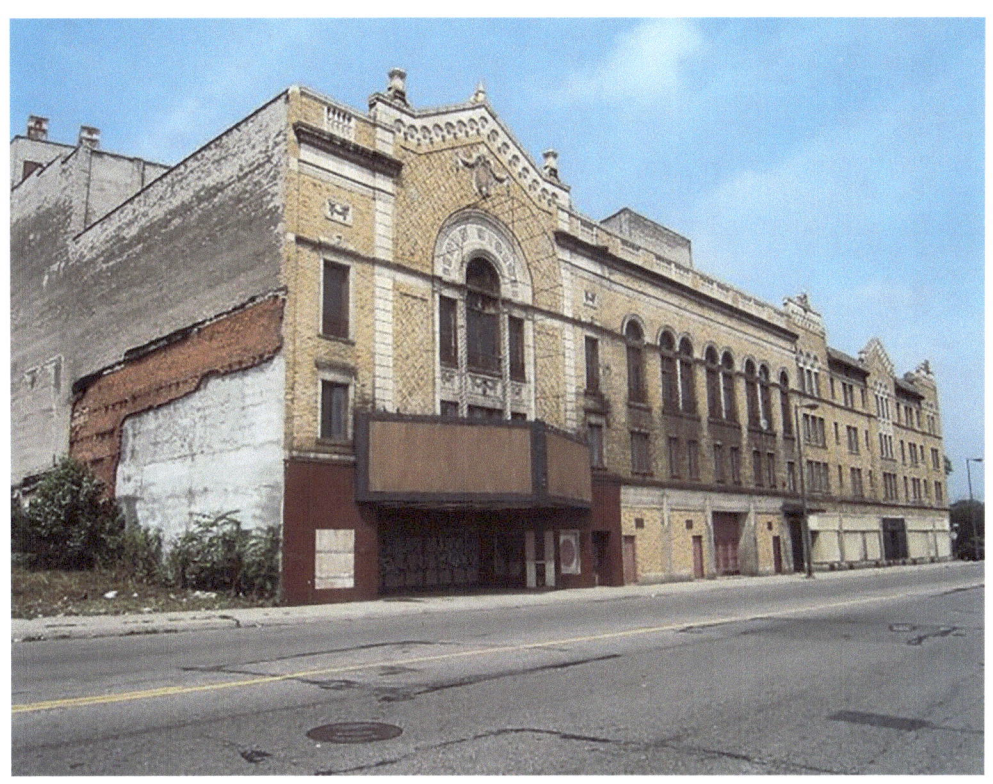

Eastville Park - Bristol, England

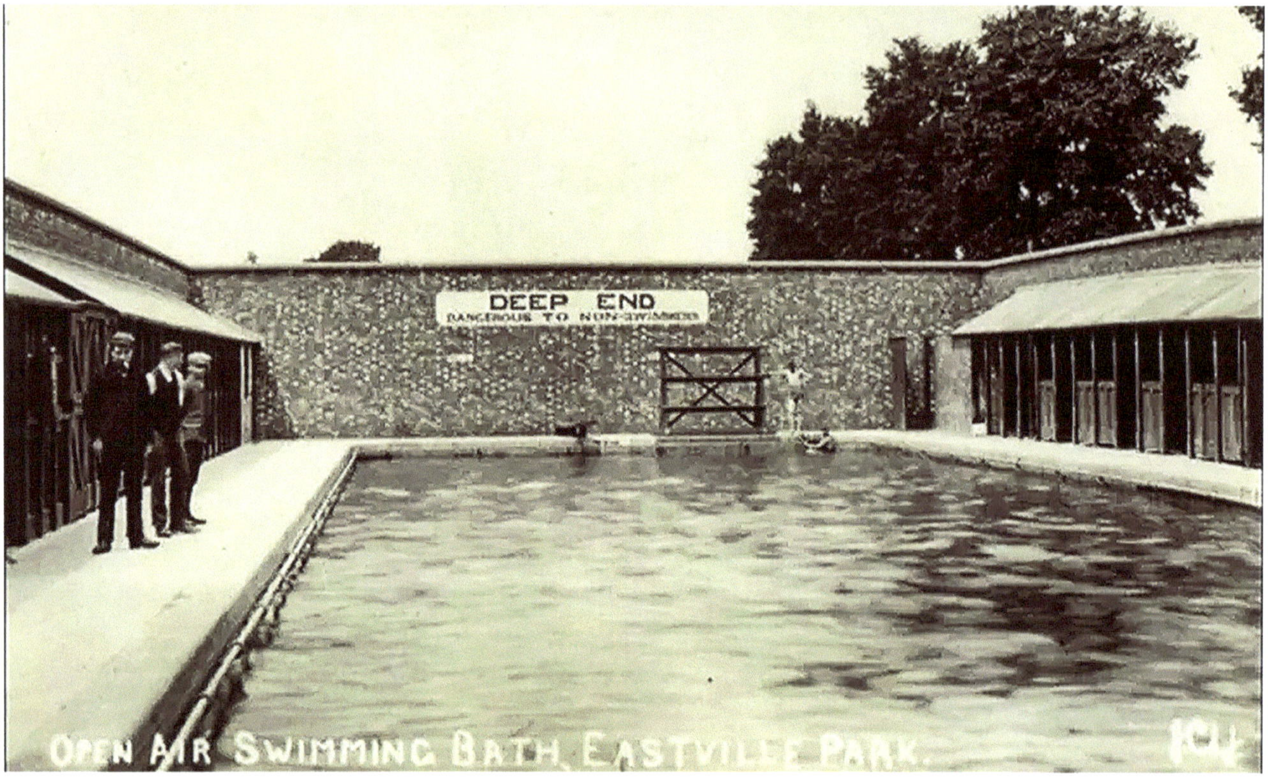

DEEP END
DANGEROUS TO NON-SWIMMERS

OPEN AIR SWIMMING BATH, EASTVILLE PARK.

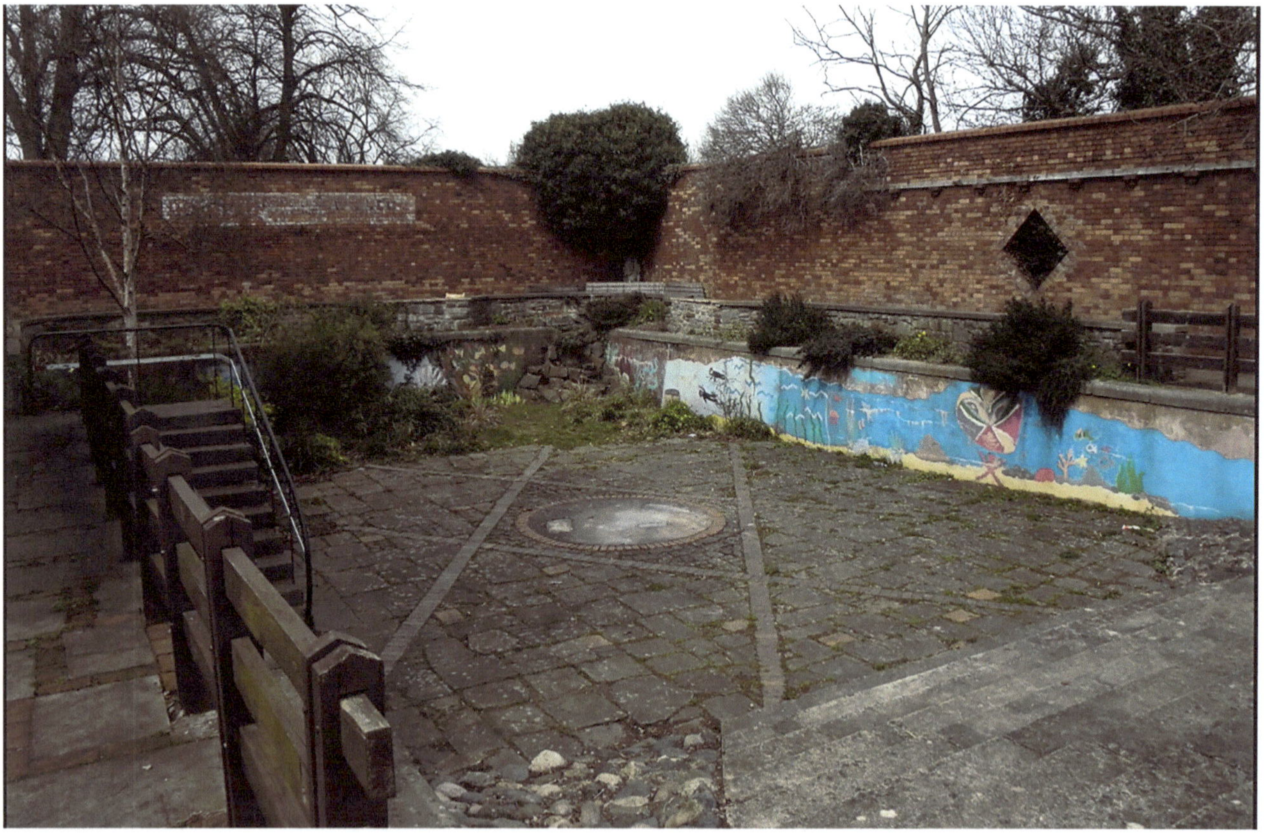

Fiddle's Dari-King - Parksville, NY

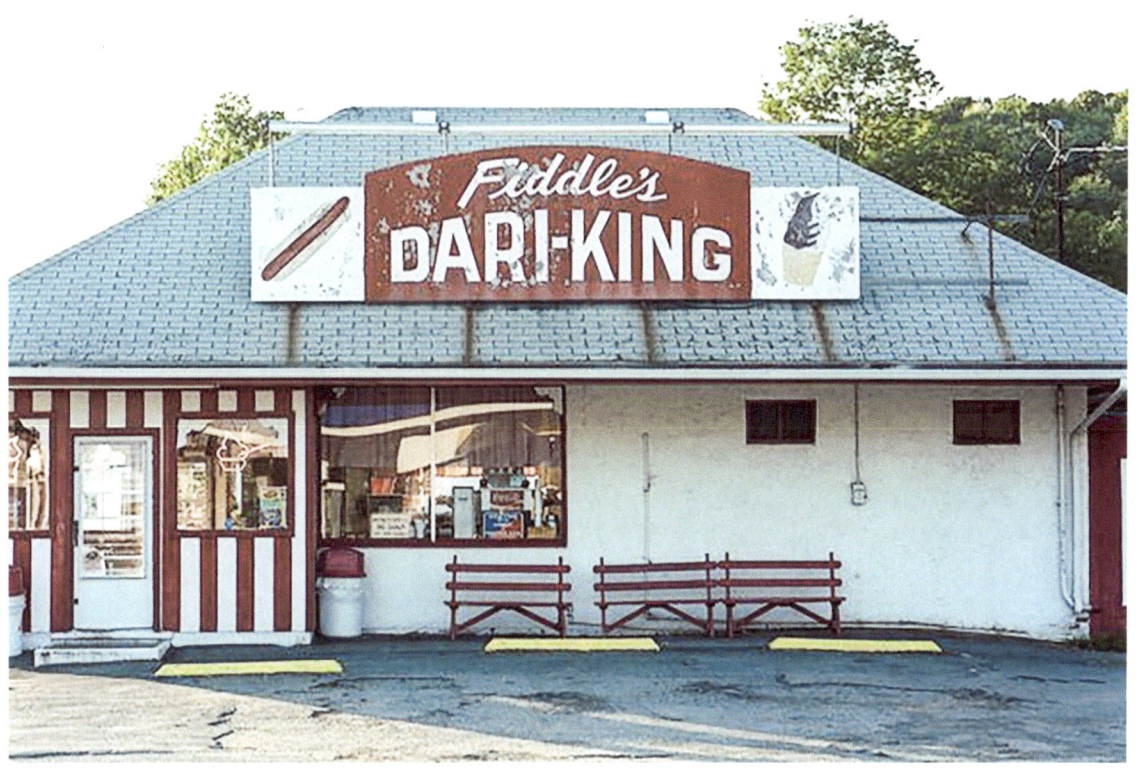

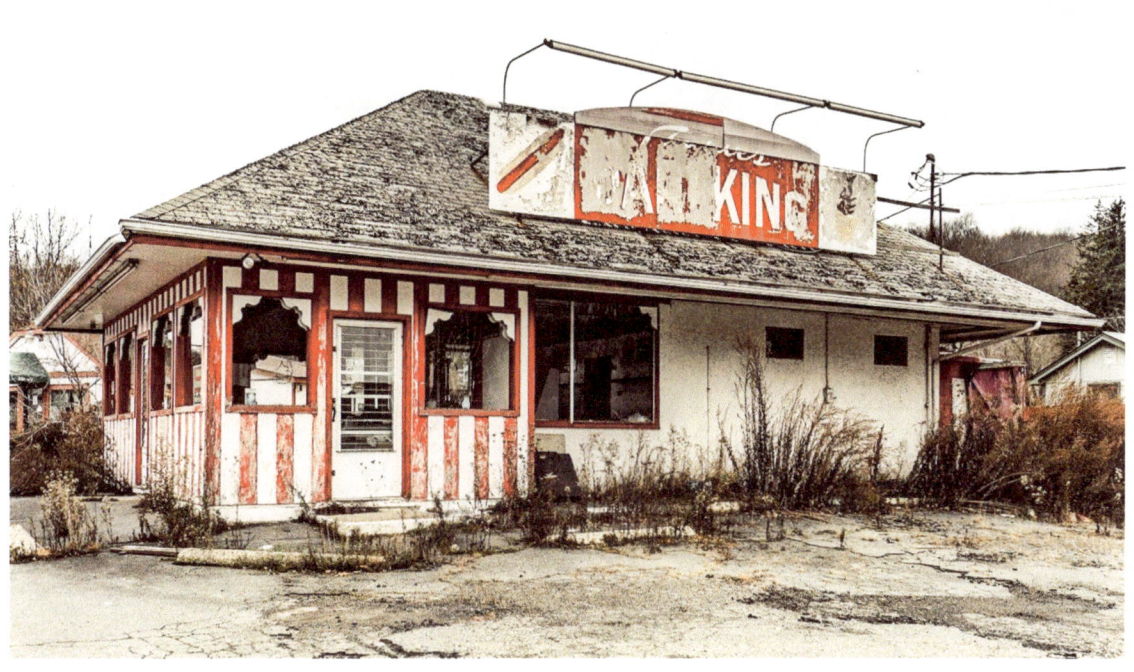

Fiesta Mall - Mesa, AZ

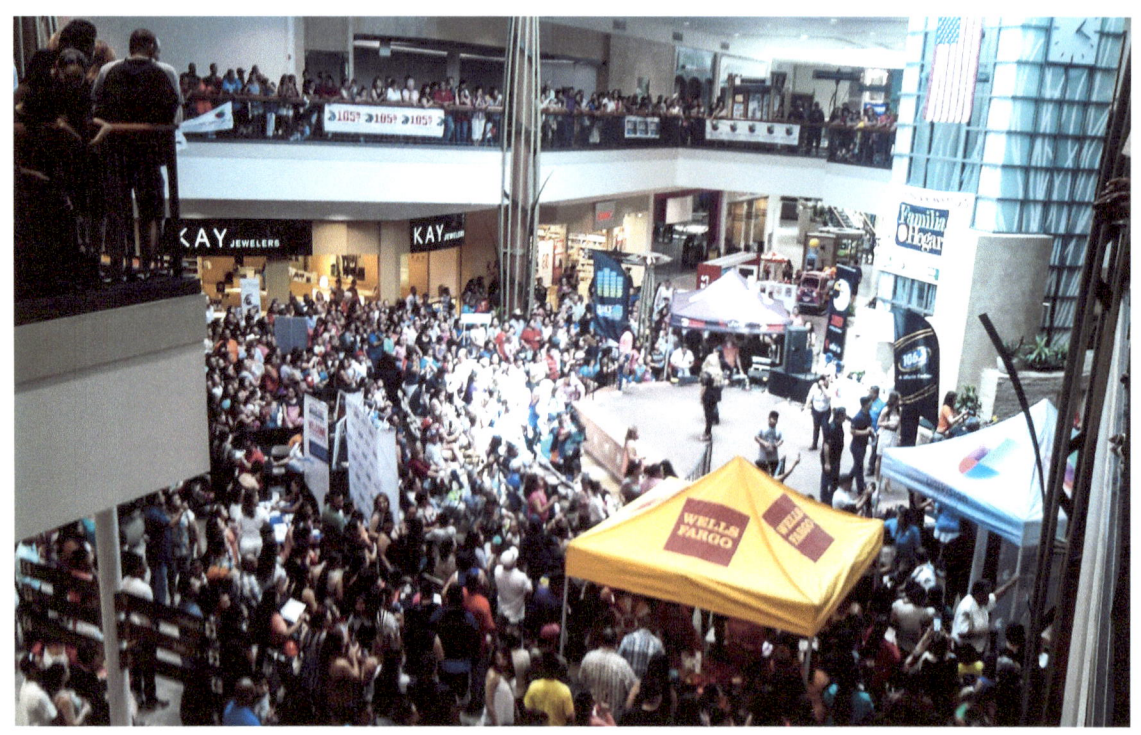

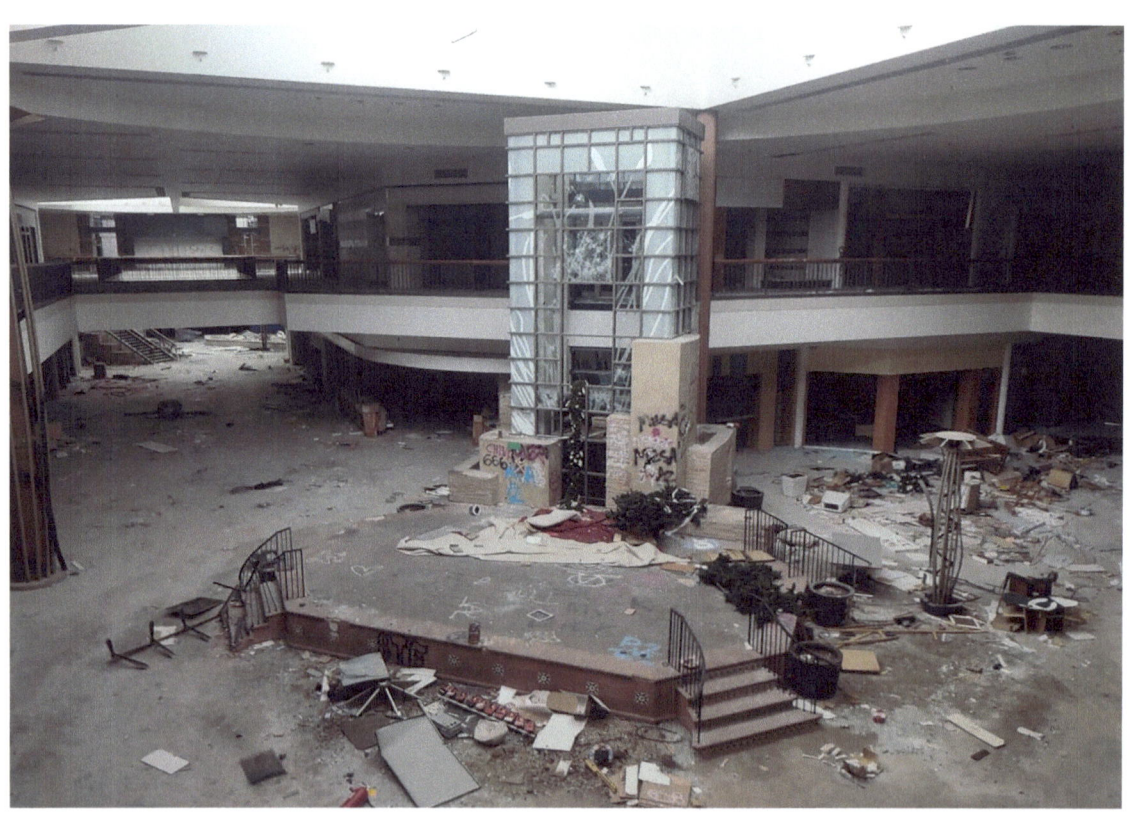

Fire House Engine House 22 - Detroit, MI

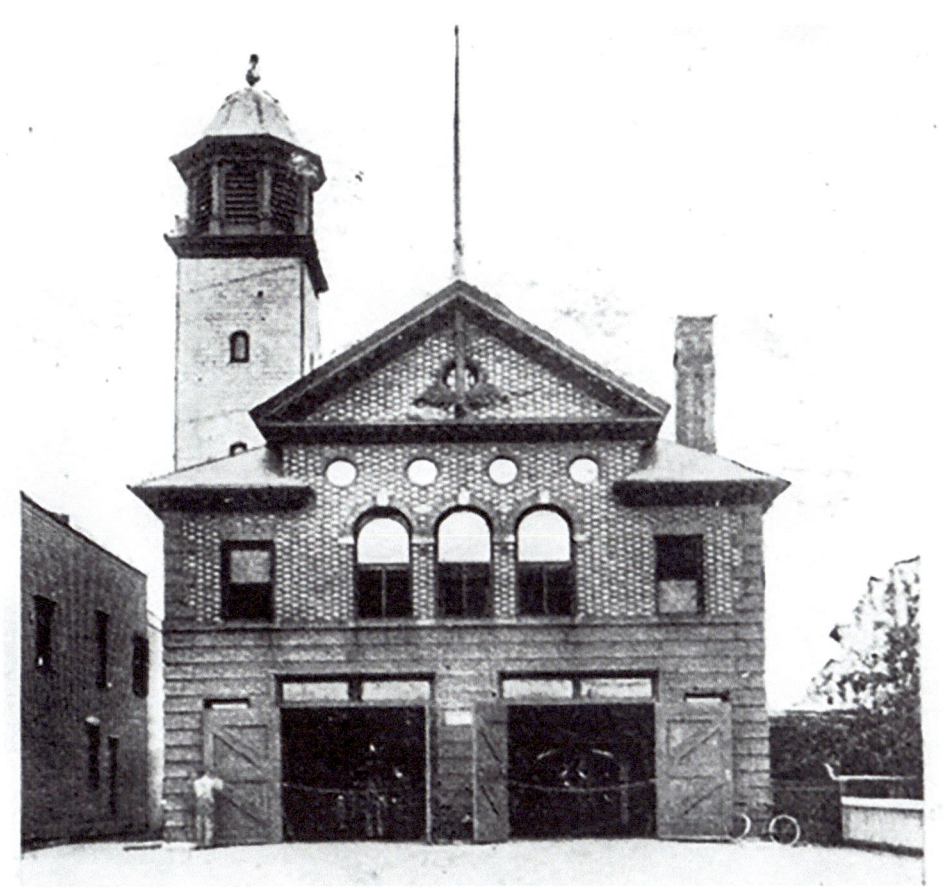

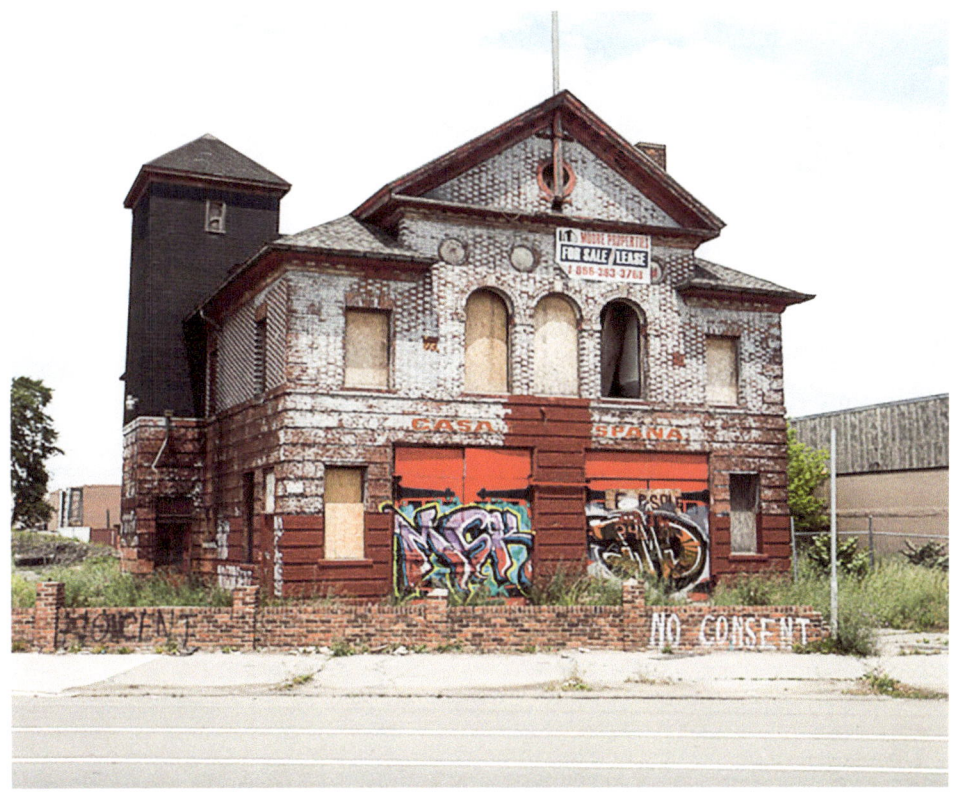

Westland Mall - Westland, MI

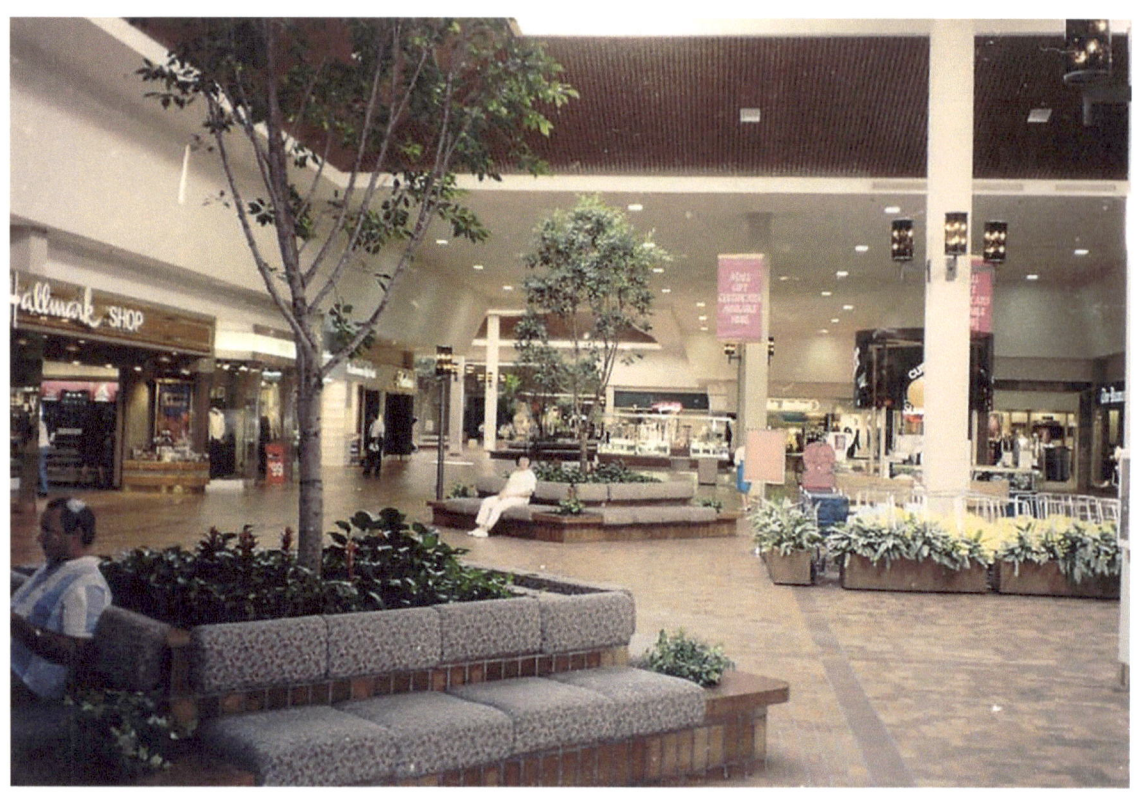

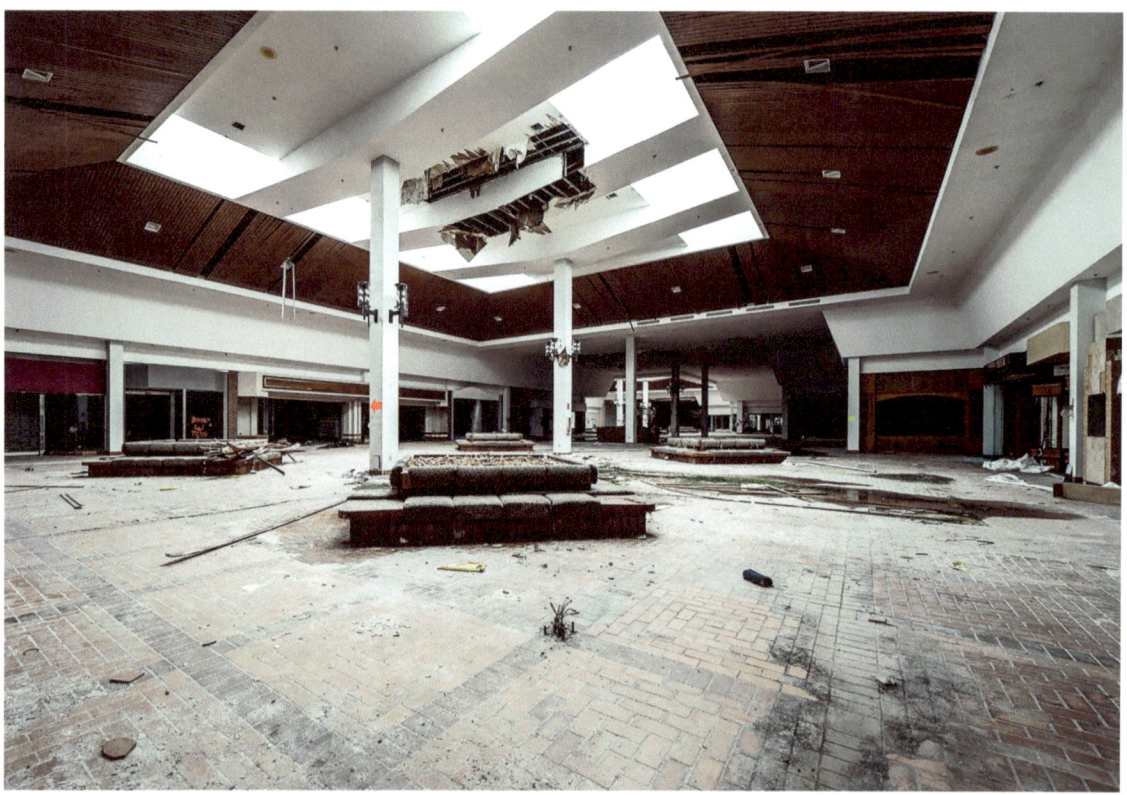

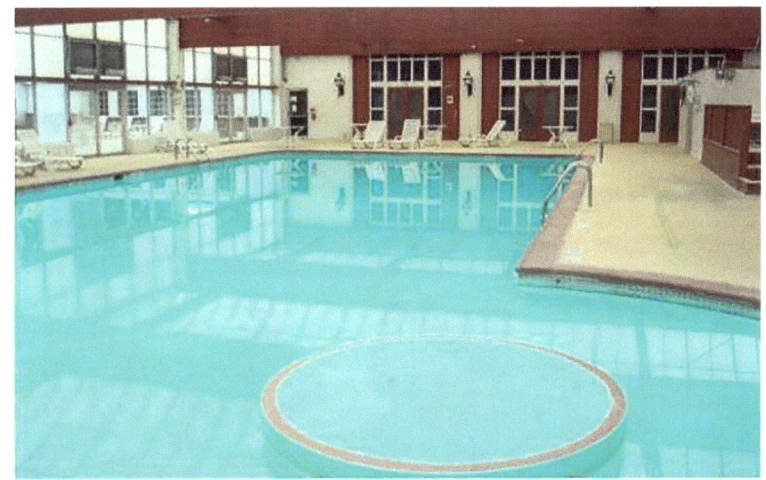

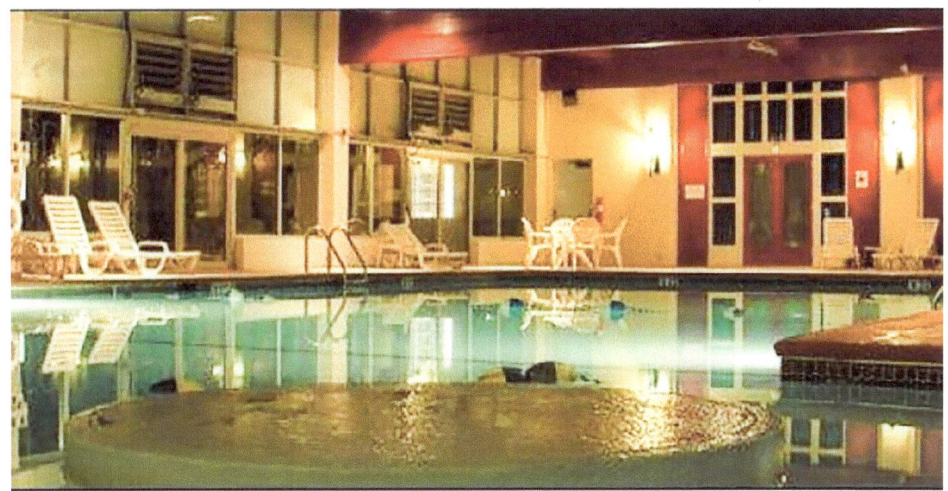

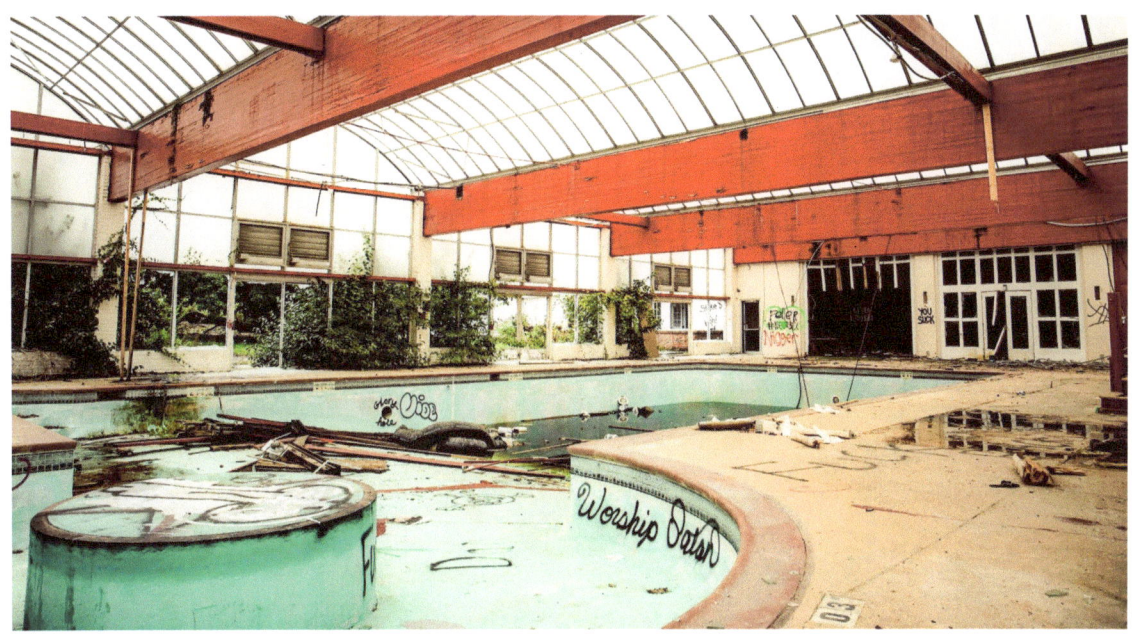

Acque della Salute Spa - Italy

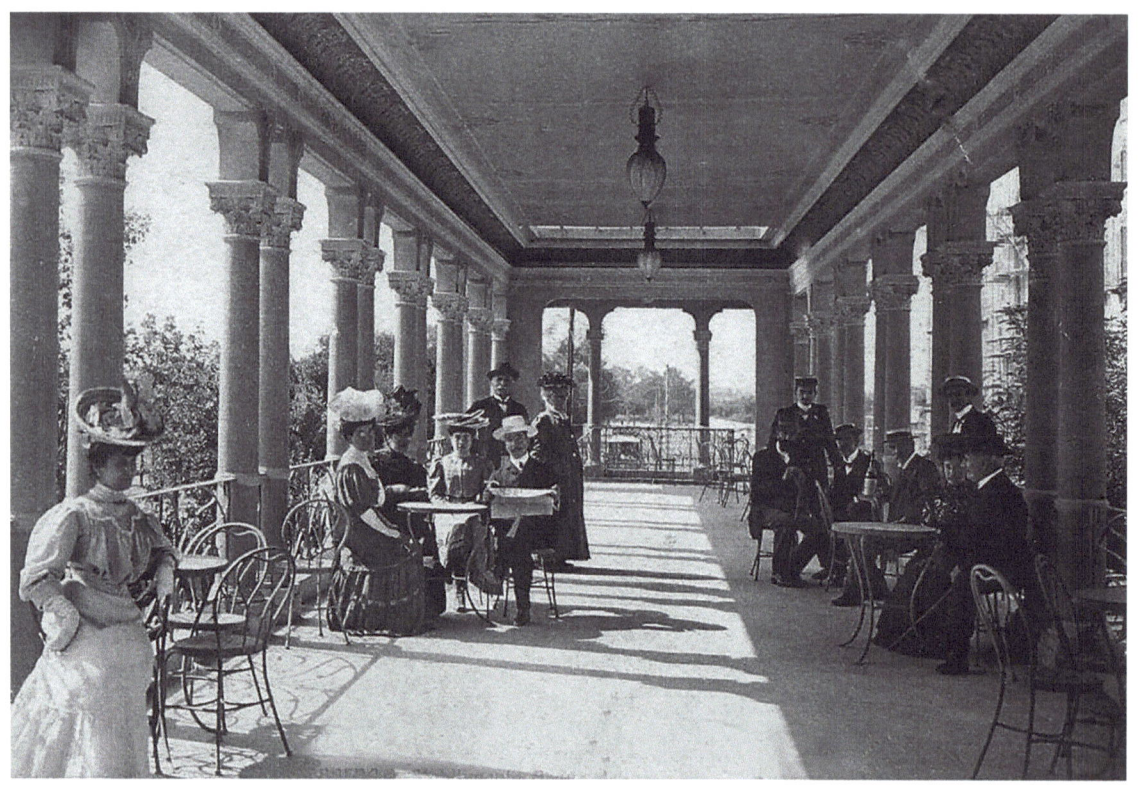

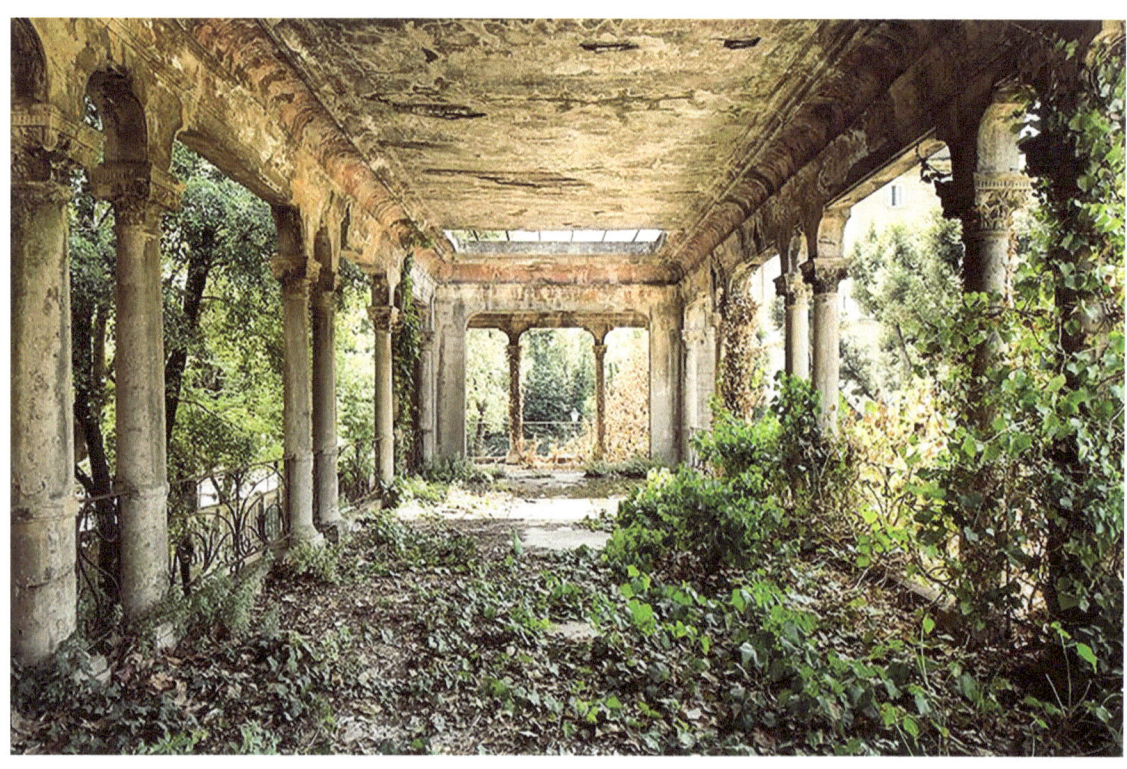

Joyland Amusement Park - Kansas

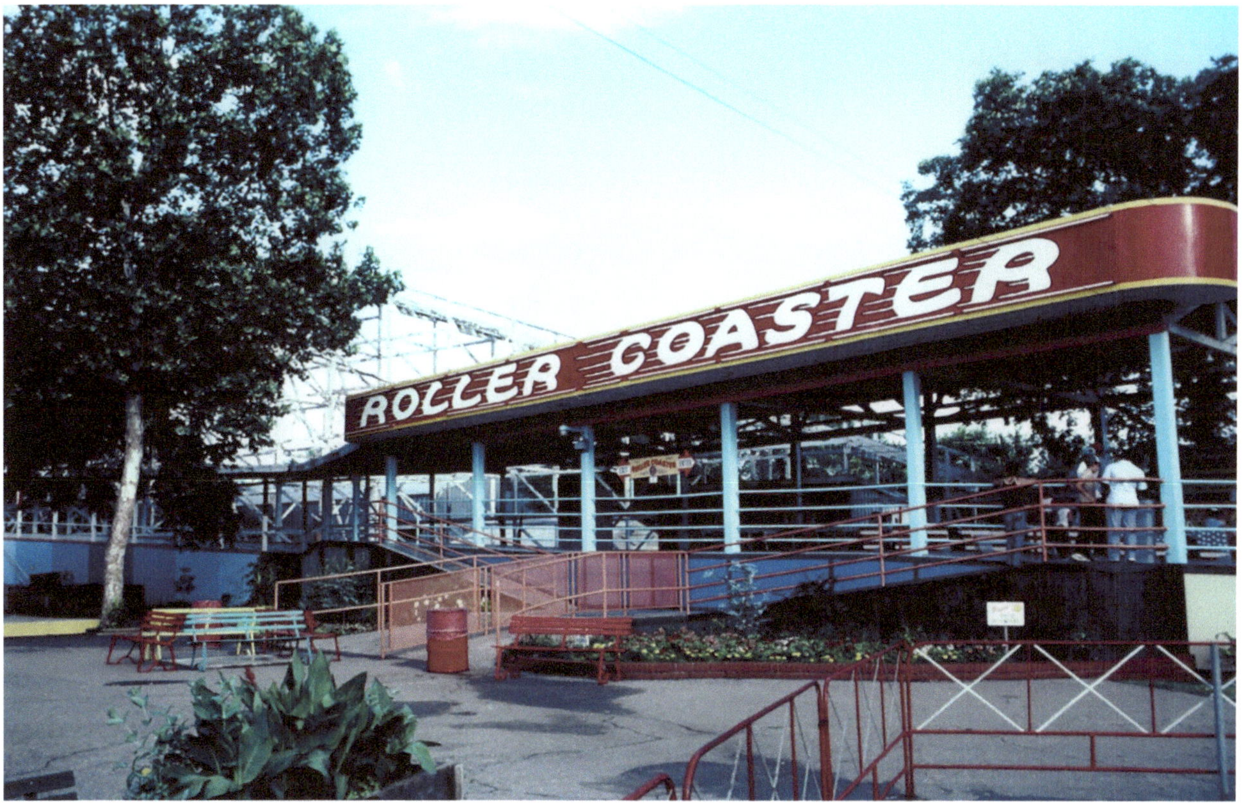

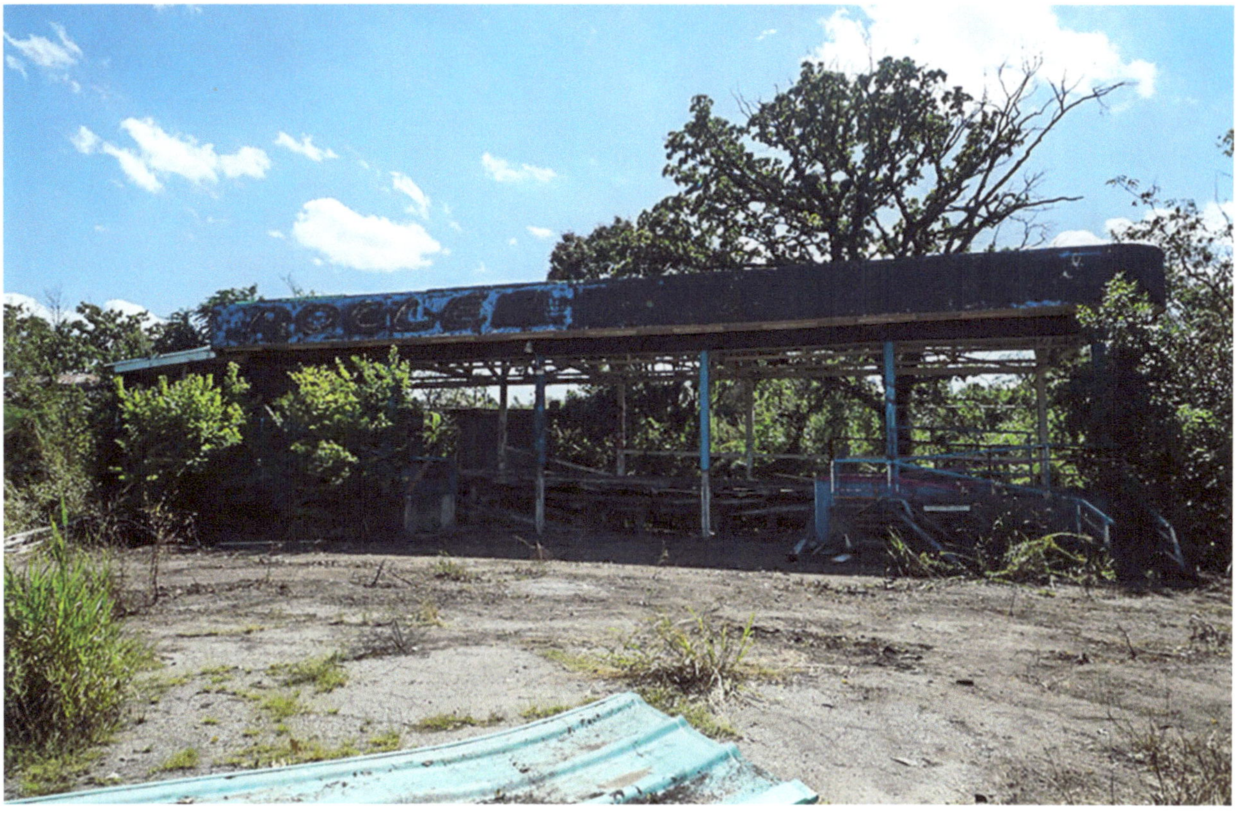

Joyland Amusement Park - Kansas

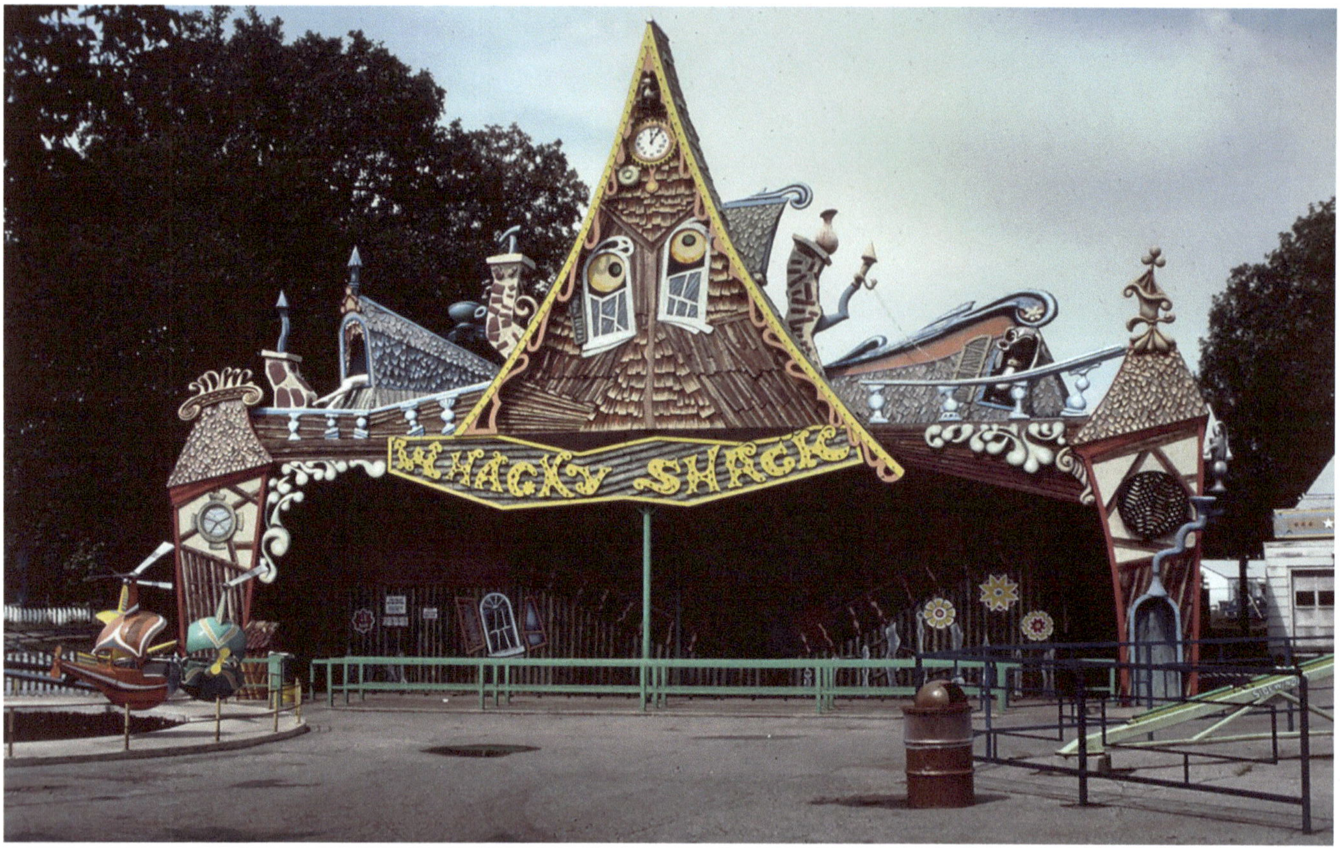

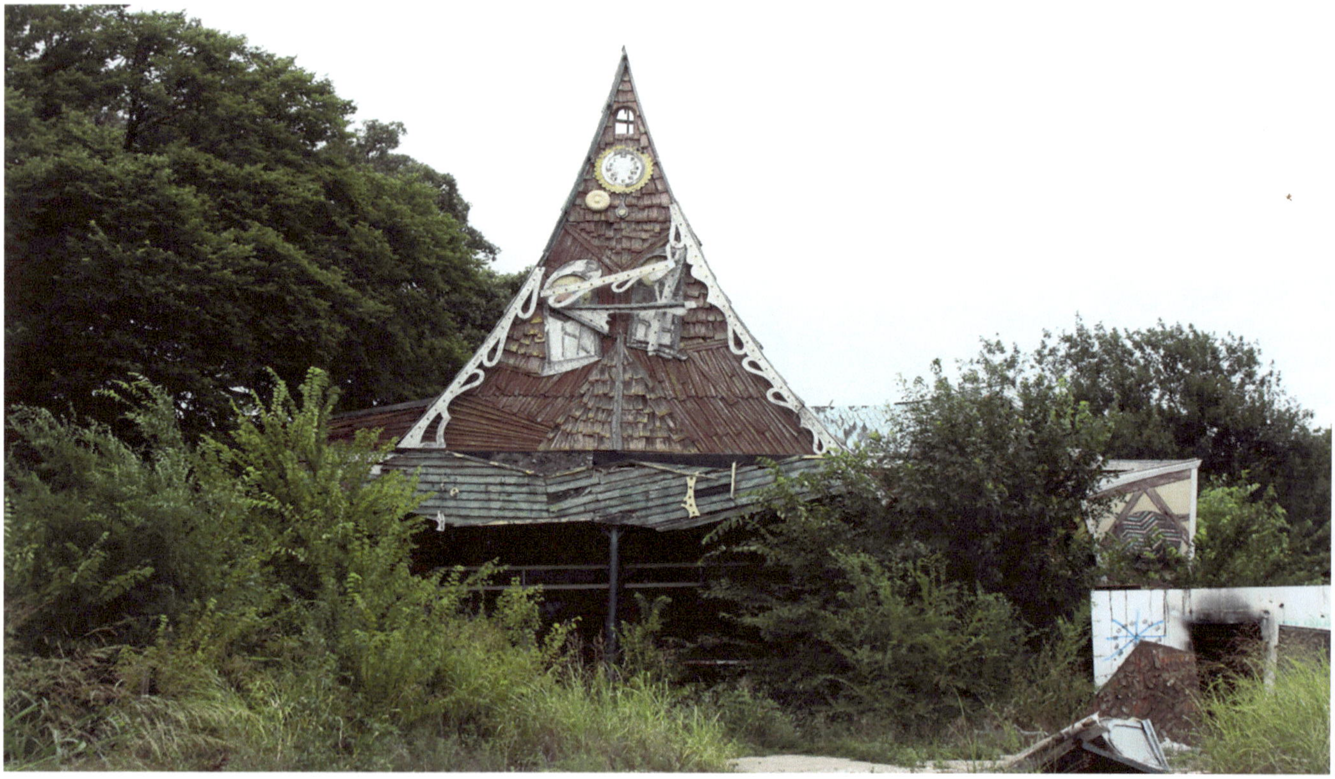

Kah-Nee-Ta Resort - Warm Springs, OR

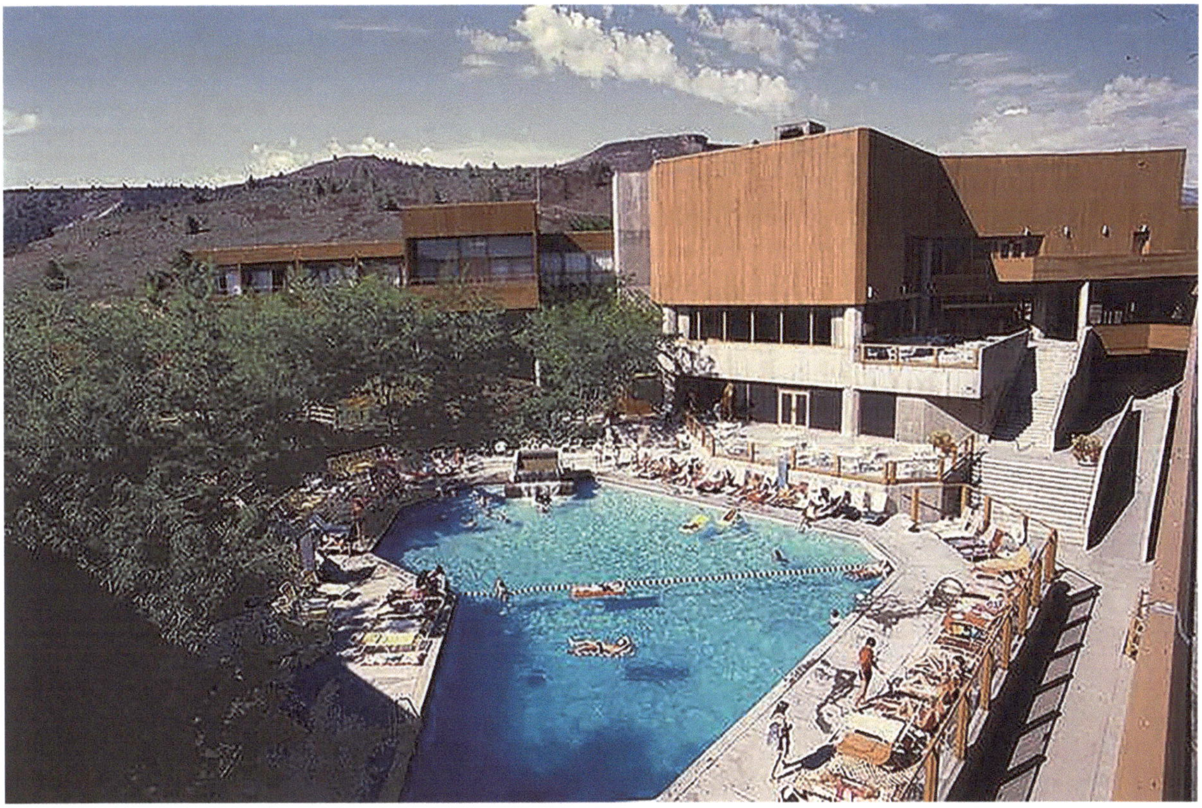

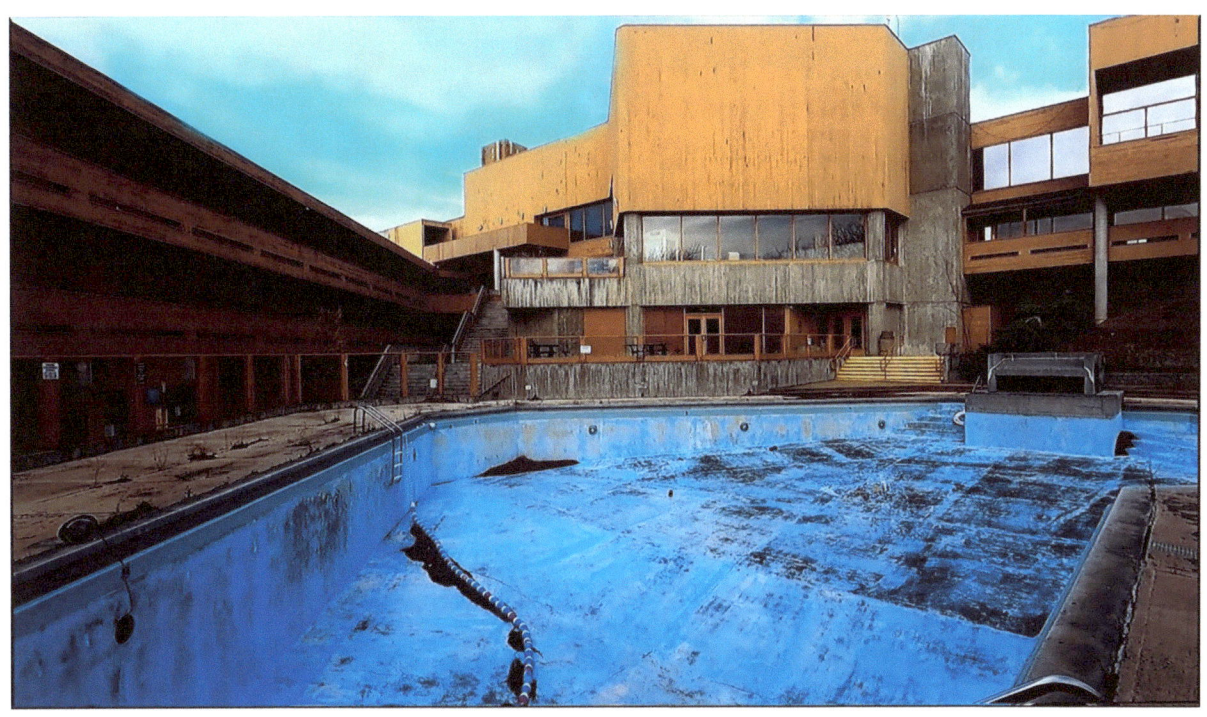

MS World Disoverer Cruise Ship -
Roderick Bay of the Nggela Islands

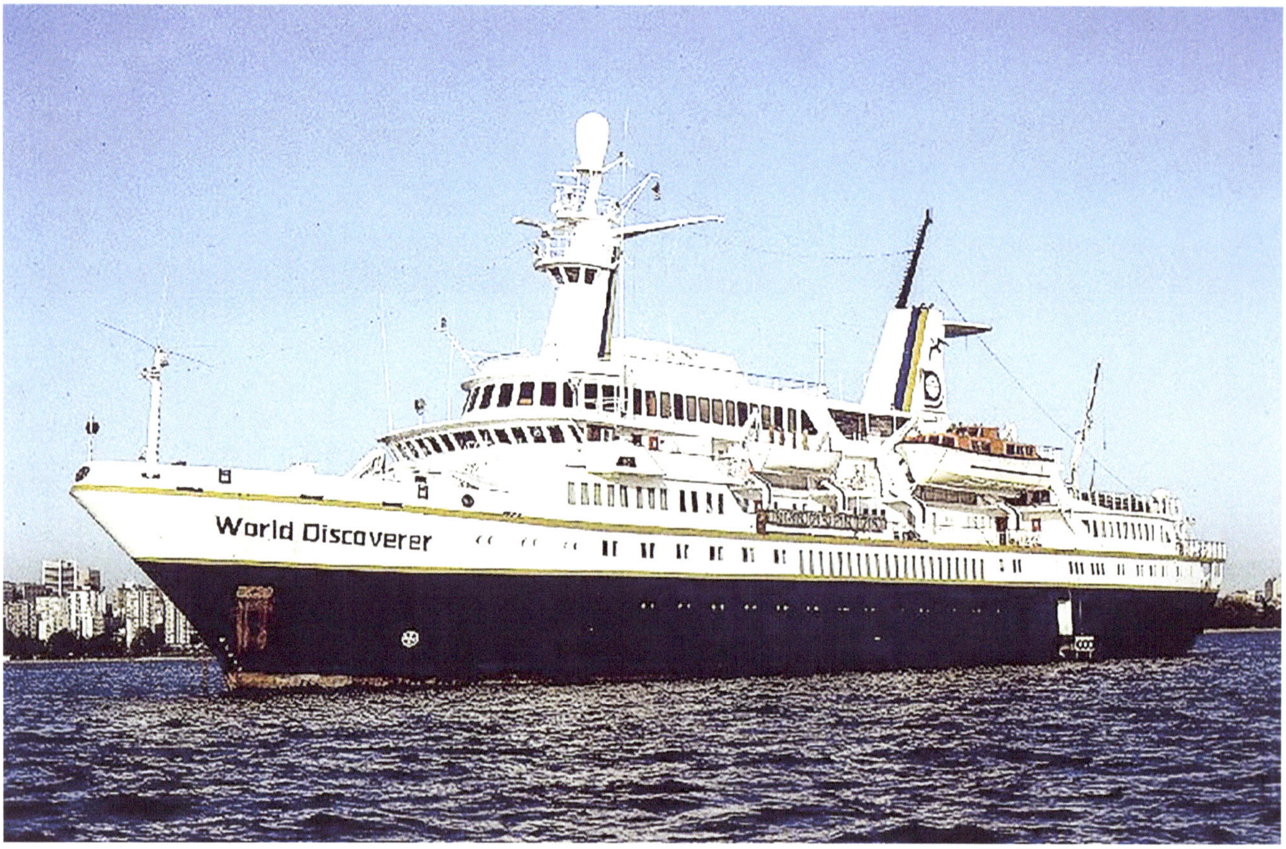

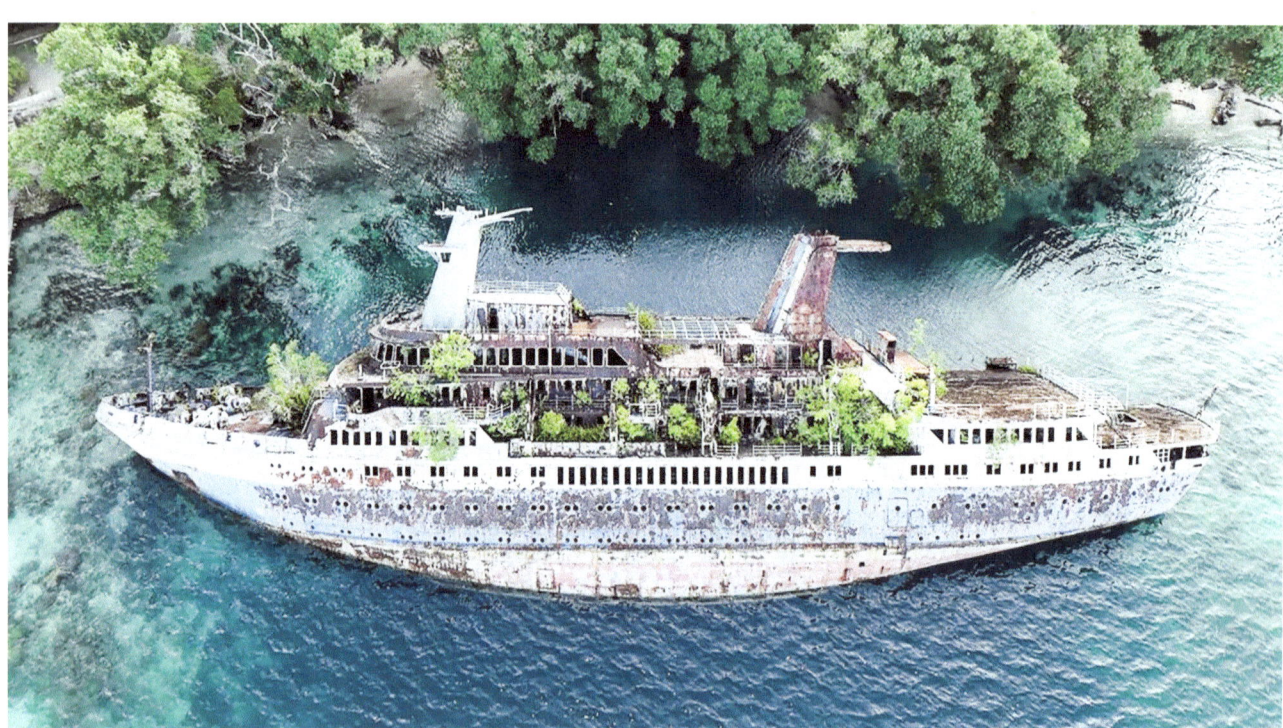

Paradise Motel & Restaurant - Cooperville, GA

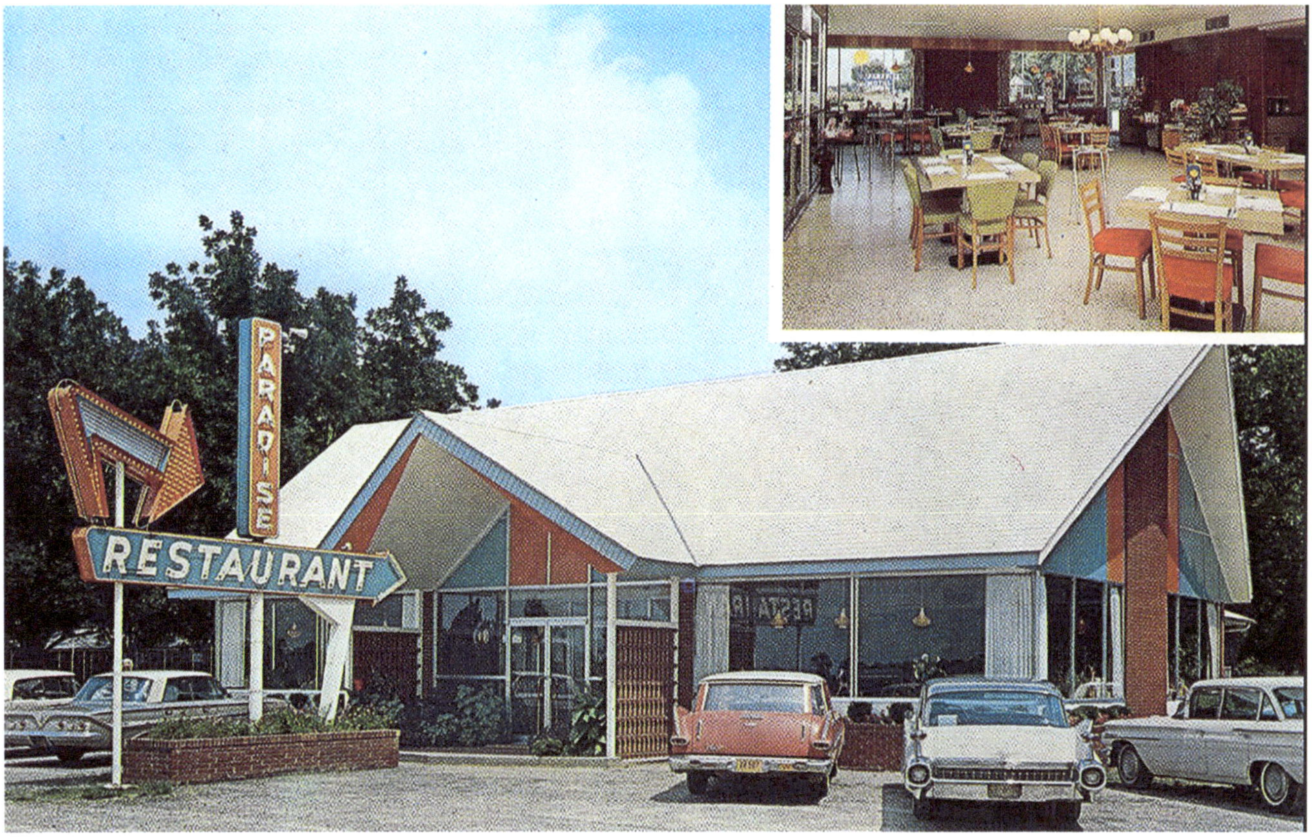

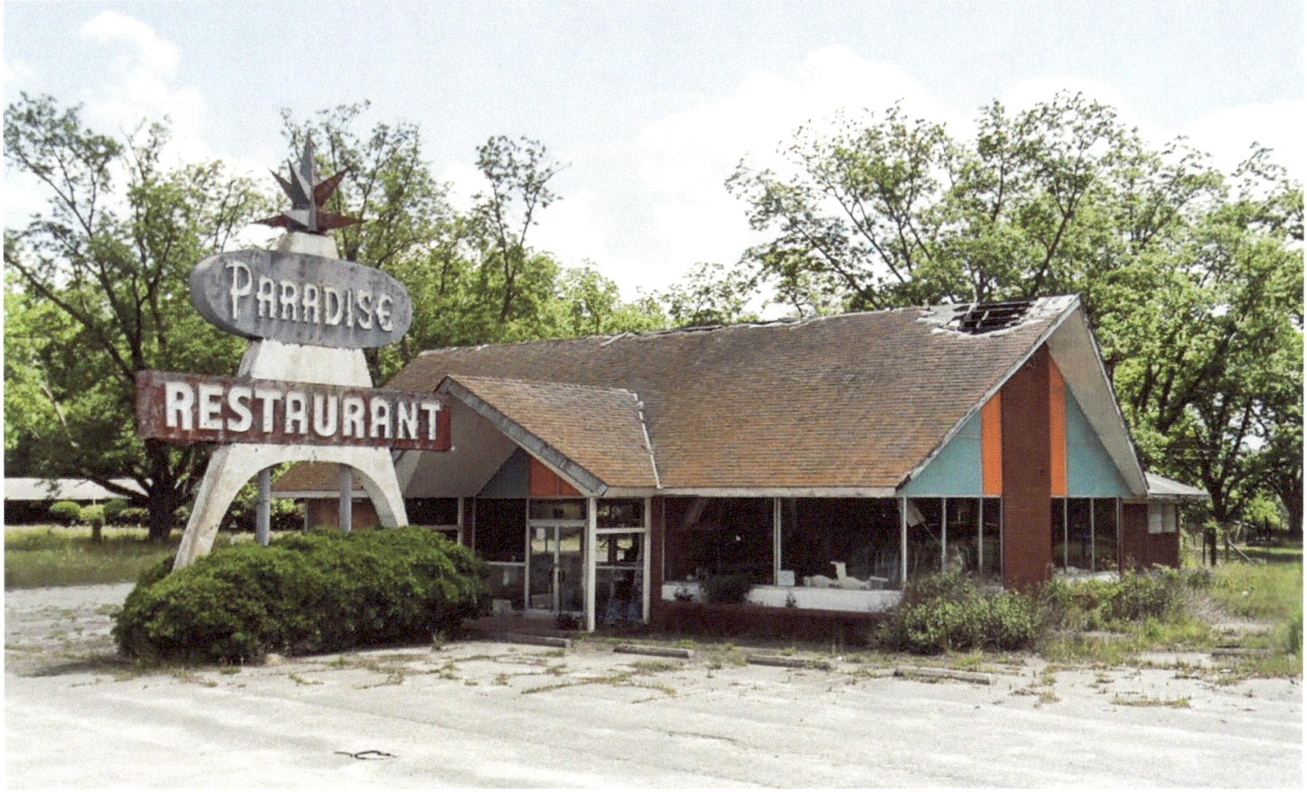

Poconos Resort Beach - New York

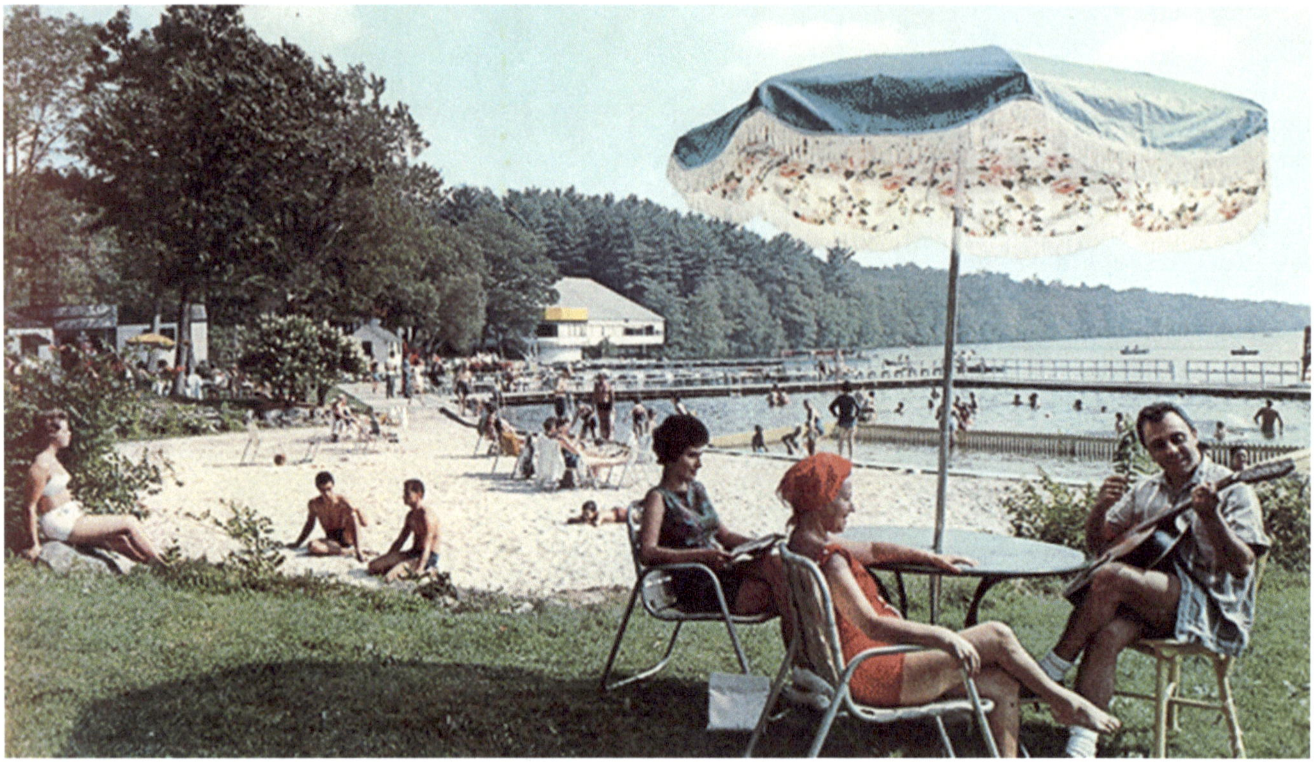

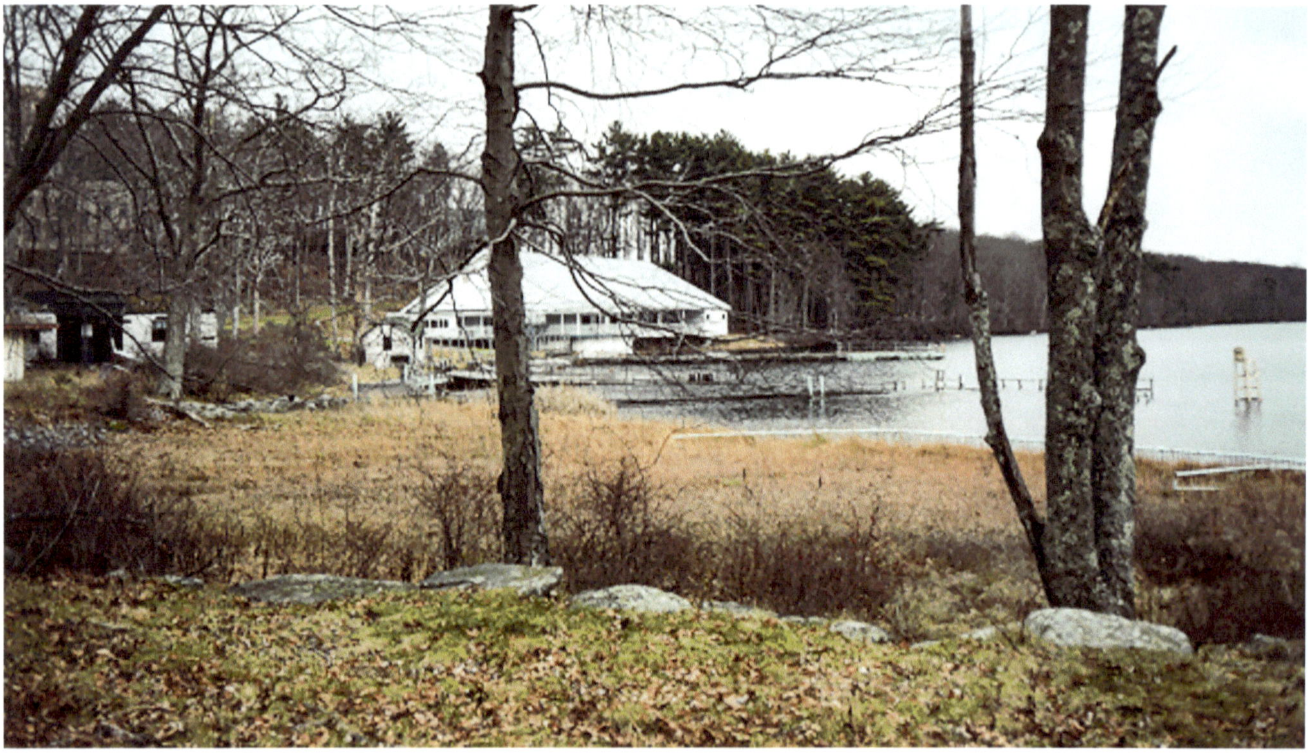

SS America Ship

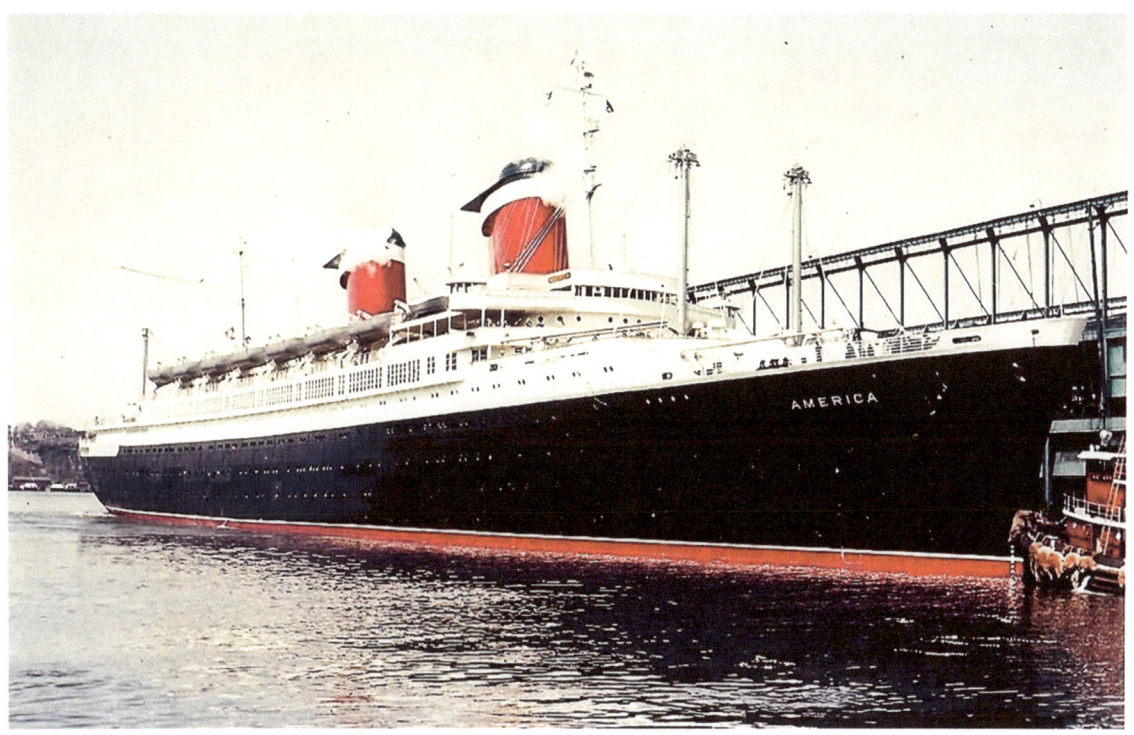

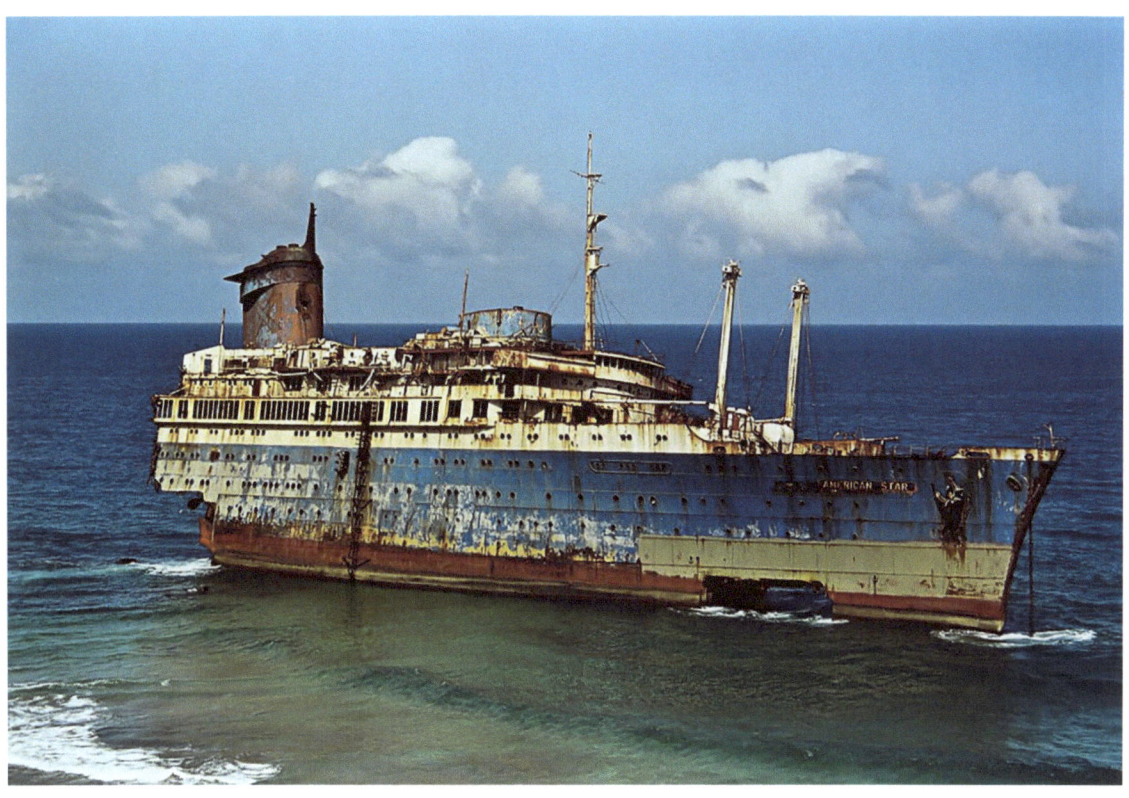

Sunrise Resort - Moodus, CT

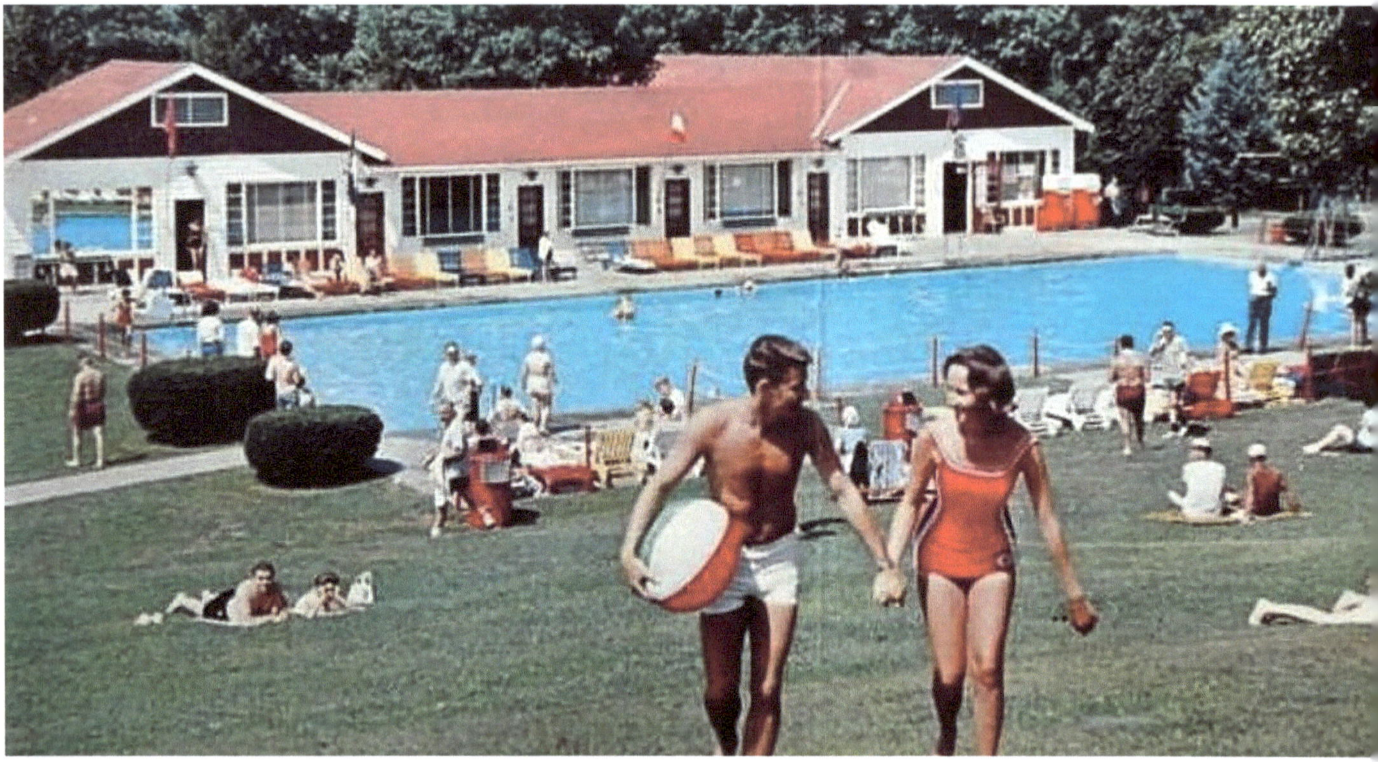

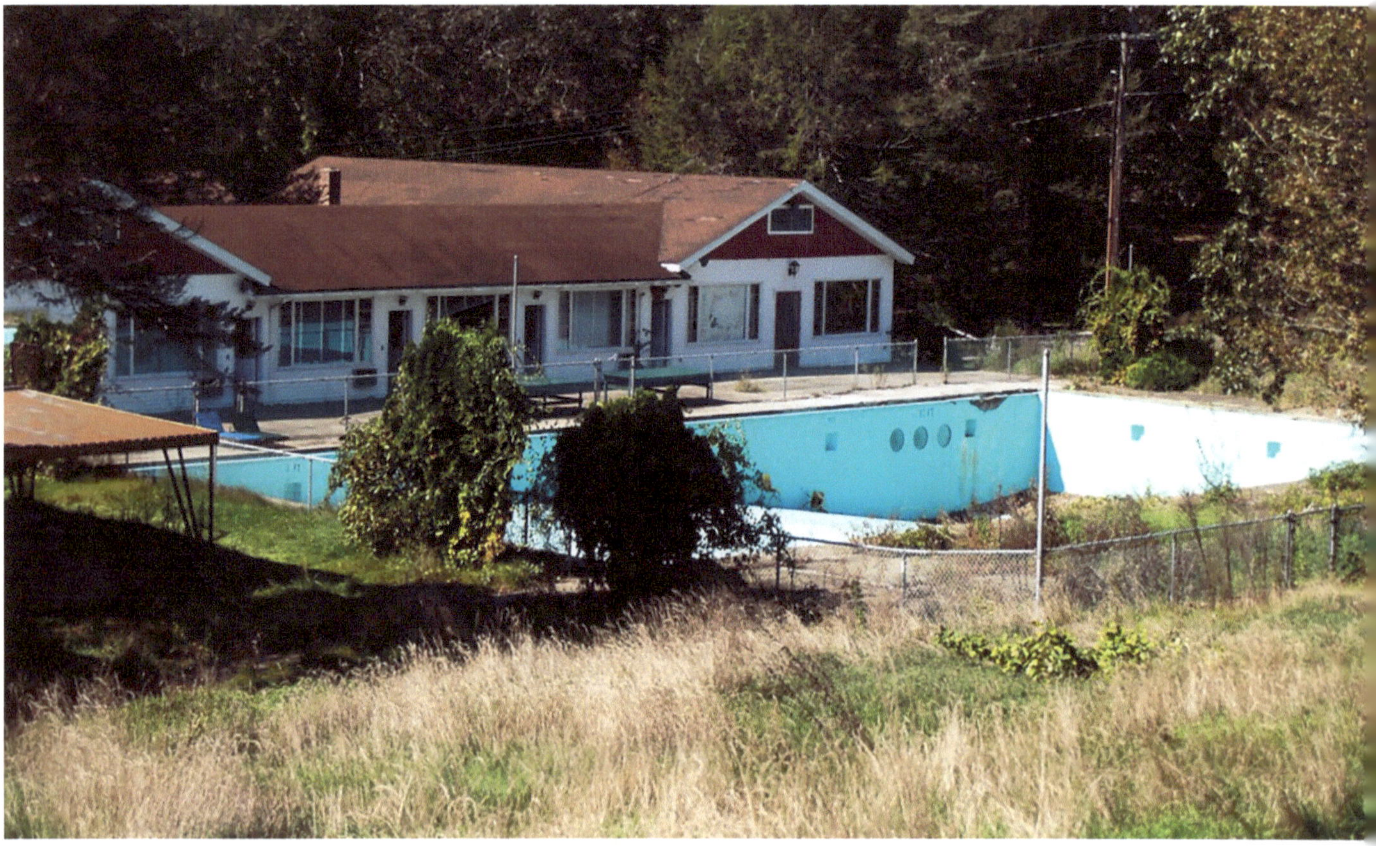

The Modernaire Motel - York, PA

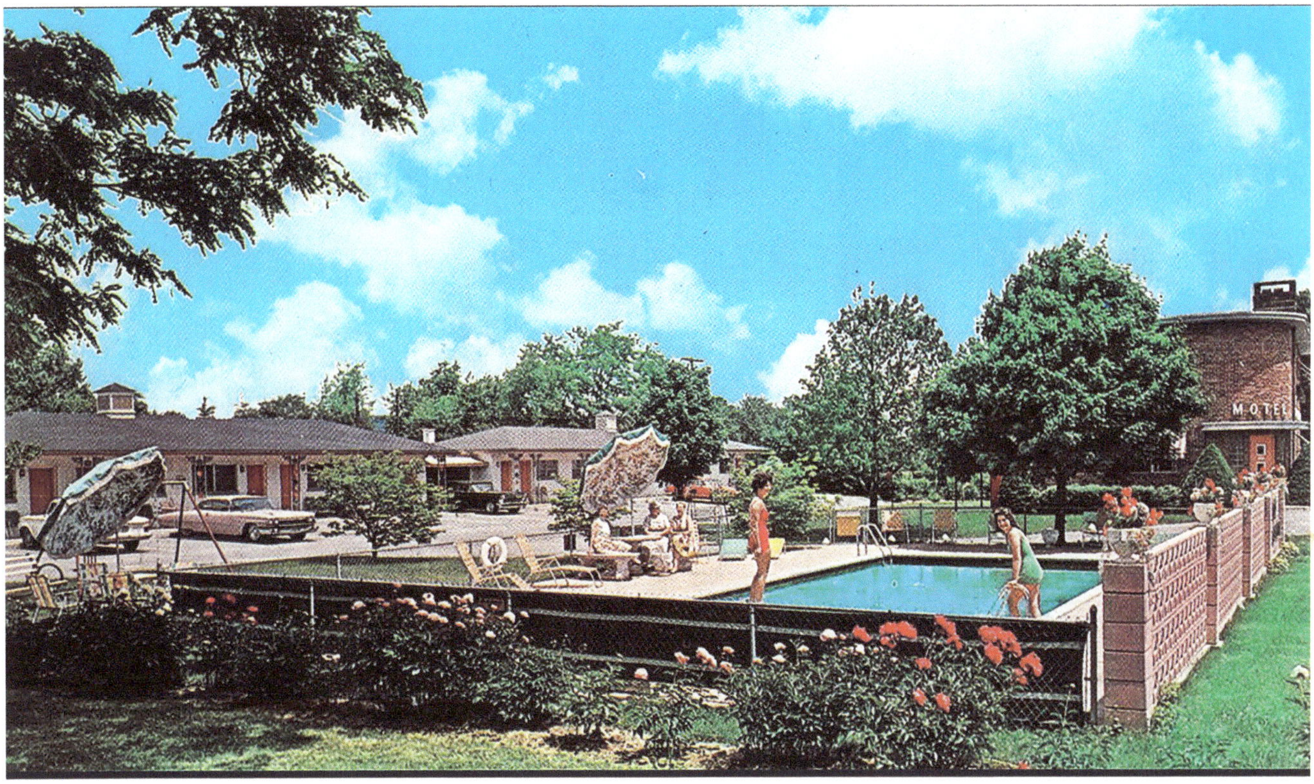

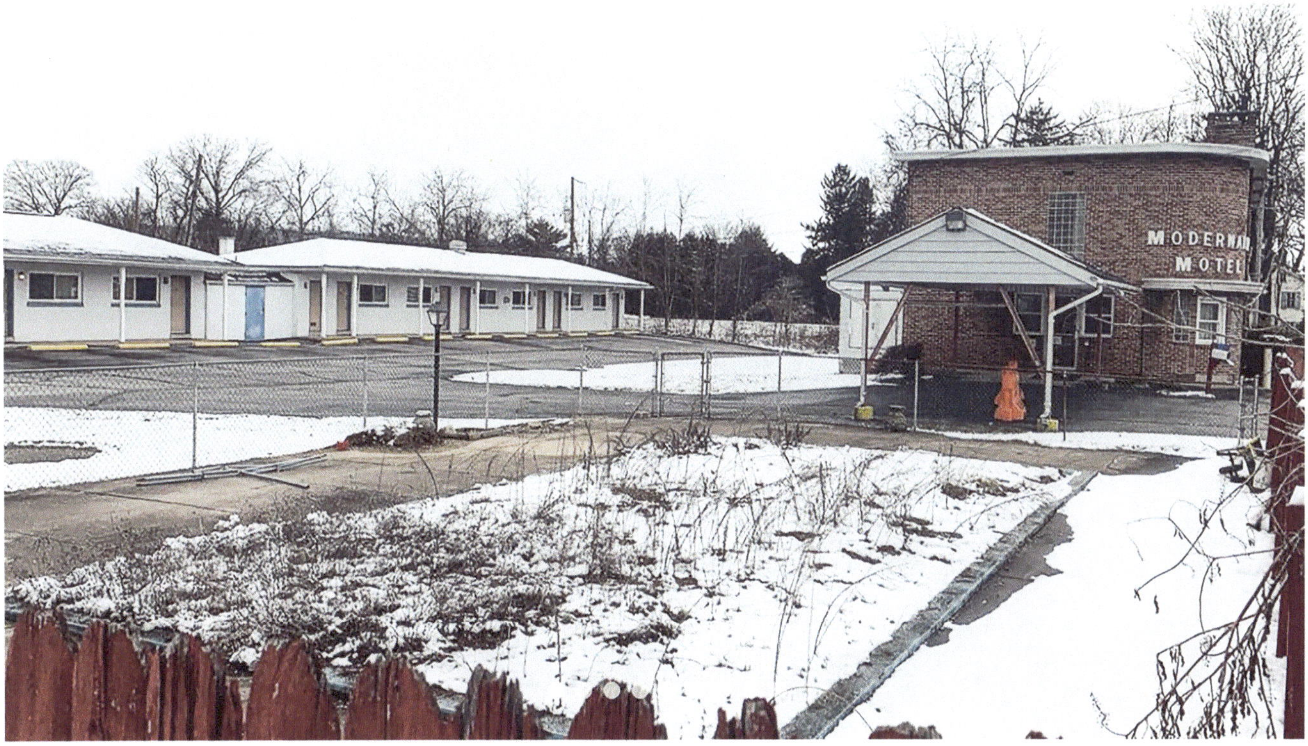

Williams Grove Amusement Park - Mechanicsburg, PA

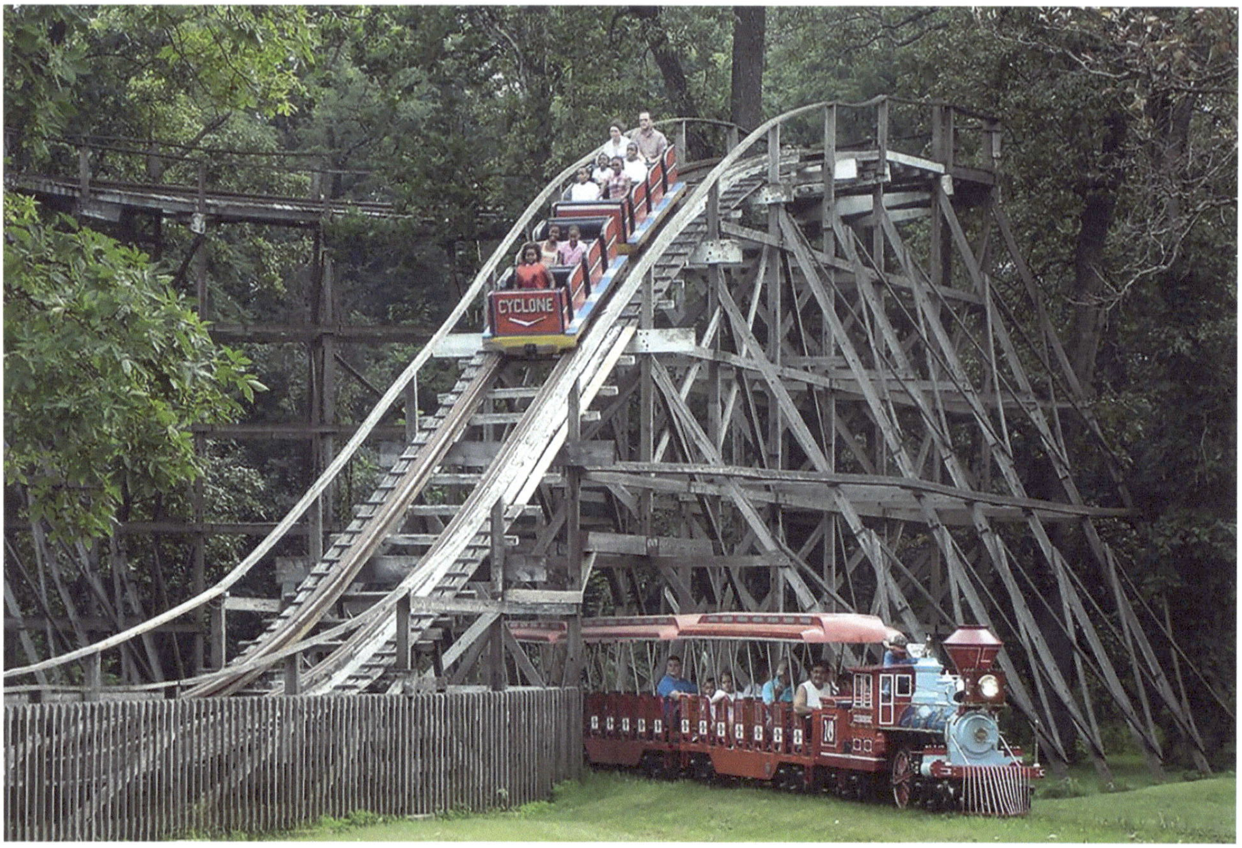

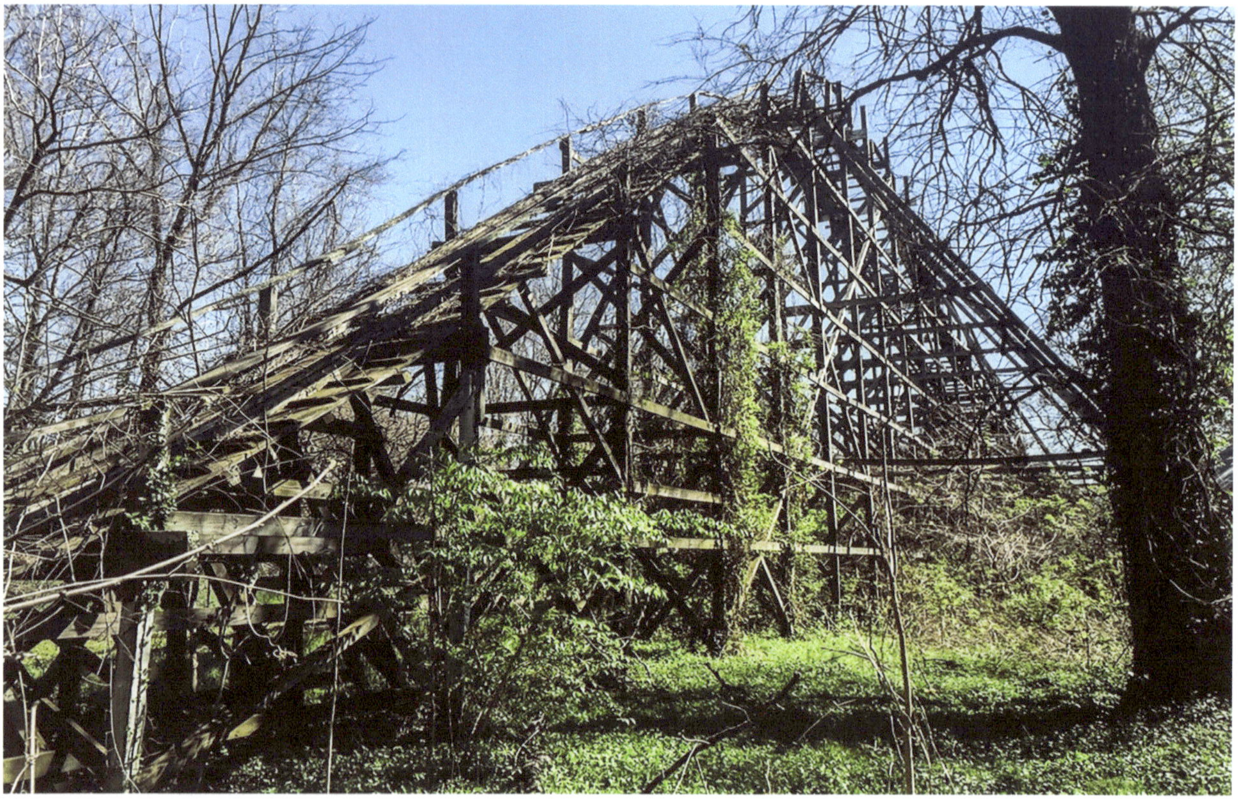